From the Reviewers

"In every leadership position, I have often found myself gasping for enlightenment, energy, and endurance long before the journey's end. Stopping to catch my breath didn't seem possible. With Scripture and story, Dave and John give us practical ways to be revived though God's life-giving breath. They show us the way to be truly alive in a world that wants to take our breath away or worse yet, make us give up."

BRAD L. HEWITT, chairman of Habitat for Humanity Worldwide

"An invitation and guide to life's most difficult, yet critical, conversation: How do I live a life of significance and meaning? Wise and practical, this book shows us how our ultimate purpose is not a good death but a good life—all the way to the very end. I recommend it to anyone who is gasping for what makes life worth living."

RICHARD LEIDER, author of *The Power of Purpose*, *Repacking Your Bags*, and *Life Reimagined*

"In this busy world that squeezes the life out of us, the only way to keep our spiritual lungs inflated is to daily inhale the life of the Spirit of God, who restores the love, joy, peace, and sound mind we so desperately need. This wonderful book will show you the way to live this reality."

JAY BENNETT, chairman of the National Christian Foundation

"In a time when humanity is in a constant state of grief, this book resuscitates the mind, body, and soul. Every story illuminates a path toward unearthing wisdom and inspiration no matter what you're facing."

NINA BOUPHASAVANH, senior writer and producer at iheartstorytelling.com

"Sooner or later we all come up gasping for breath. David and John will masterfully help you recover your breath and come alive. It's compelling. It's convicting. No impotent religion. They invite you to experience something special."

GAIL & JOCK FICKEN, executive leaders of PLI

"The thought of *Gasping for Breath* is such a powerful and transcendent example of what all of us inevitably experience in life, whether in business, in relationships, or physically. Best yet, it has a gravitational pull to the truth of a spiritual life. A must-read!"

BRIAN SLIPKA, CEO of True North Equity Partners and founder/president of Slipka Foundation

"As a certified spiritual director, I have the privilege of listening with men and women who are 'out of breath' and struggling to stay engaged in the stories of their lives. This book will be a gift to anyone who finds themselves in a similar place. Dave and John offer practical ways to breathe deeply of God's Spirit and be fully alive right in the midst of the challenges we face."

VICKI DEGNER, former pastor of spiritual development at Church of the Open Door

"If you find yourself silently overwhelmed and secretly searching for a way out, *Gasping for Breath* offers a refreshing alternative: learning to stay in it for the long haul without losing your soul. Dave and John are seasoned leaders who offer hard-won wisdom to help you navigate your own journey of recovering your breath and coming alive."

STEVE WIENS, author of *Beginnings*, *Whole*, and *Shining Like the Sun*

"For decades I've watched Dave lead, teach, preach, and love from a thirsty heart for the *now* presence of the kingdom. In my estimation, he and John had to write this book. It's long overdue and desperately needed by all of us right now . . . today. We need a deeper breath."

REV. MICHAEL PASCHALL, author of *Till Death Do Us Part* and *Raw Talks of Wisdom*

"Dave and John invite us to rediscover real life, animated by the Spirit of God. They write not from the ivory tower of pristine theological reflection, but as fellow 'gaspers' whose real and raw insights were refined in the fire of their own desperation. Read this book slowly and prayerfully. I believe that God will use this to restore the souls of many who are running out of breath."

MIKE LUEKEN, senior pastor of Oak Hills Church and coauthor of *Renovation of the Church*

"Busacker and Johnson breathe wisdom into a world gasping for truth. Their deep and wise perspective makes this a must-read for an unhinged world. It is a critical blueprint to remaining grounded in these untethered times."

PHILIP STYRLUND, CEO of The Summit Group and author of *Relevance*

"Dave and John know well the painful realities of this world that can shrink our souls and harden our hearts. They also know how to encounter the true God who is greater and more beautiful than any thought or word we could use to describe Him. *Gasping for Breath* helps us imagine a life lived in the reality of God's presence and ever-active kingdom in a God-breathed world."

KENT CARLSON, founding pastor of Oak Hills Church and coauthor of *Renovation of the Church*

"With a message more urgently needed today than ever, Johnson and Busacker address what it means to be truly alive—to live, renew, grow, and thrive in a world where we can never catch our breath. Their book instructs us in how we can gain or regain the spiritual aliveness that comes from receiving the breath of God. A must-read."

MICHAEL W. ANDERSON, LP, coauthor of *Gist: The Essence of Raising Life-Ready Kids*

"With grace, sensitivity, and irreverent humor, Johnson and Busacker provide the source of hope we all so desperately need with vivid imagery and candid first-person insights. We are all out of breath . . . and most of us don't even know it!"

WARD BREHM, philanthropist and recipient of the Presidential Citizens Medal for his work in Africa

Gasping for Breath

INVITING GOD'S SPIRIT INTO YOUR OVERWHELMED LIFE

DAVID JOHNSON
JOHN BUSACKER

Emerald Books

P.O. BOX 635,
LYNNWOOD, WA 98046

Published by Emerald Books
P.O. Box 635
Lynnwood WA 98046
800-922-2143
www.EmeraldBooks.com

ISBN 978-1-62486-146-8 (paperback)
ISBN 978-1-62486-147-5 (ebook)

Printed in the United States of America

Scripture quotations that are not noted with a Bible version are paraphrased.

Scripture quotations noted NASB are taken from the *New American Standard Bible*®, Copyright © 1960, 1962, 1963, 1968, 1971, 1972, 1973, 1975, 1977, 1995 by The Lockman Foundation. Used by permission.

Scripture quotations noted NIV are taken from *The Holy Bible, New International Version*® NIV®. Copyright © 1973, 1978, 1984, 2011 by Biblica, Inc.™ Used by permission. All rights reserved worldwide.

Scripture quotations noted NKJV are taken from the *New King James Version* of the Bible. Copyright © 1982 by Thomas Nelson, Inc. Used by permission. All rights reserved.

Scripture quotations noted NLT are taken from the *Holy Bible, New Living Translation*, copyright © 1996, 2004, 2007 by Tyndale House Foundation. Used by permission of Tyndale House Publishers, Inc., Carol Stream, IL 60188. All rights reserved.

Scripture quotations noted MSG are taken from *The Message*. Copyright © 1993, 1994, 1995, 1996, 2000, 2001, 2002. Used by permission of NavPress Publishing Group.

Scripture quotations noted THE VOICE are taken from the *The Voice*. Copyright © 2012 Thomas Nelson, Inc. The Voice™ translation © 2012 Ecclesia Bible Society. All rights reserved.

Scripture quotations noted ESV are taken from the *Holy Bible, English Standard Version*®. Copyright © 2001 by Crossway, a publishing ministry of Good News Publishers. ESV® Text Edition: 2011. Used by permission. All rights reserved.

Literary development: Lance Wubbels Literary Services, Bloomington, Minnesota.
Cover and typesetting: Andrew Kaupang, andrewkaupang.com

Dave Johnson

To the congregation, elders, and staff
at Church of the Open Door,
who for thirty-eight years gave me room
to grow, change, and breathe.

Like me, they were flawed and faithful,
grumpy and grateful, irritating and delightful,
in daily need of grace but eager to dispense it—
of such are the kingdom of heaven.
I am eternally grateful!

John Busacker

To my now departed mom and dad,
for loving me enough to plant tiny seeds of faith
from the time I was a little boy.

Those seeds were watered by the tears of everyday life,
nurtured by the love of wise mentors,
called out by the curiosity of small group friends,
challenged by the demands of bottom-line business leaders,
shaped by the instruction of gifted teachers,
prayed over by my loving wife, and
protected by the love of my ever-present Father.

Those little seeds are finally maturing into a tree.

It just took a little time!

About the Authors

DAVID JOHNSON is a pastor, author, and speaker who served as senior pastor at Church of the Open Door in Minneapolis, Minnesota, for thirty-eight years. His deep commitment to biblical integrity along with a capacity to communicate it clearly with an unvarnished style has made him a sought-after speaker both nationally and internationally.

David's undergraduate work at Bethel University was followed by postgraduate work at Trinity Evangelical Divinity School. He is the author of *The Subtle Power of Spiritual Abuse* and *Joy Comes in the Mourning* and is presently the founder and executive director of Things That Remain.

Though living in Minneapolis since 1980, David and his wife, Bonnie, grew up in Chicago and remain "fully devoted followers" of the Cubs, Bears, Blackhawks, and Bulls. They have four grown children and ten fabulous grandchildren.

JOHN BUSACKER is a writer, speaker, and entrepreneur. He is the founder of *Life*-Worth, a leadership development and life planning consulting firm. He has delivered presentations, facilitated workshops, and orchestrated conferences on six continents, engaging such issues as personal leadership, authentic faith, and holistic generosity.

His groundbreaking *Leadership Studios* curate inspiring environments, subject matter expertise, and experiential service learning into a transformational development journey for men and women desiring to steward their life and leadership with wisdom and intentionality.

John is the author or coauthor of several books, including *do less, be more: The Life-Changing Power of Focus*, *Dare to Answer: 8 Questions That Awaken Your Faith*, and *Inspiring Generosity: Stories of Faith and Grace in Art*.

John's passion for people extends globally, supporting the development needs of leaders with a variety of nonprofits and faith-based organizations in the U.S. and sub-Saharan Africa.

He and his wife, Carol, live outside Minneapolis, Minnesota, and have two married children and three exuberant grandchildren.

Acknowledgments

Dave: This book would never have happened without the vision and support of my friend and coauthor, John Busacker. He woke up one day with what felt like a vision, then shared it with me when we met for lunch. It didn't take long for me to see what he saw. For nine months we collaborated, got discouraged, saw the light, lost our way, found it again, and kept believing that what we were trying to say might matter. John kept telling me that I was the golfer and he was the caddie—he was wrong about that!

For my wife in particular, who had to live with me while I wrote this book, during a pandemic, dealing daily with my IPF, disappearing into my *cave* for hours on end, and for pulling me out of that *cave* in just the nick of time—I just think you're the best. Thank you for your patience, and sometimes for losing your patience at just the right time.

John: In the acknowledgments of *Fully Engaged*, a book I wrote in 2011, I thanked "My new and cool friend, Dave, whose unvarnished input has provoked belly laughs and whose divine teaching has caused my faith to grow more in one year than in the previous twenty-five." I had no idea then that God had it in mind to grow our friendship, those laughs, and that teaching into this book nine years later. Our friendship has deepened, we've continued to laugh heartily, and the last nine months writing with Dave has exponentially expanded my faith again.

And for Carol, who knows me through and through, still loves me, and is inexhaustibly patient during the seasons when I go off and write for hours. Thank you for calling out the very best in me as a husband, friend, father, and grandfather. I'd probably settle for less. You'll have none of it!

Dave and John: Our editor, Lance Wubbels, came along at just the right time, and we couldn't be more grateful. Not just good at what he does, Lance believed in the message of this book and helped us see things we couldn't see and say things we wouldn't have thought to say without him. What the book morphed into when Lance got involved was often stunning to us. Thank you, Lance.

Thank you to Ken Finsaas, who introduced us to Jim Parrish, who introduced us to Lance Wubbels—just at the right time.

For Mike and Steve, who helped us think through publishing, and for Warren at Emerald Books as well as Andy, our typesetter and cover designer, who made it all look good—we are truly grateful for all of you.

The support and encouragement from the board of Things That Remain is invaluable. For Jason, Vicki, Ned, Ken, Paul, and Bonnie, we are truly grateful.

And for all of our friends and family who read the rough drafts and pretended to like it. Actually, I think you did like it, at least some of it, and at times it kept us going. Thanks!

Contents

Introduction

*D*ave: The test results had been emailed to us, and though written in a language only doctors understand, we knew that this time they had found something significant. So when I stepped into the doctor's office for the follow-up explanation, I felt a strange mixture of both hope and fear, of both longing and dread.

I'm glad my wife, Bonnie, was there when we heard the full diagnosis. Not just for the support, but her presence helped make it feel real as the doctor's words hung in the air like a fog that left me feeling a bit dizzy and disoriented—the whole thing felt surreal.

But at the same time, and this is kind of crazy, I had a strange sense of relief when the doctor explained what was wrong with me, because someone finally named it. The shortness of breath, the chronic cough, and the fatigue that accompanied them both could no longer be explained away. It wasn't exercise-induced asthma. Another inhaler wouldn't help.

When he showed me the CT scan and called it IPF, I was relieved. Tired of being told it was "nothing," someone finally said it was "something"—and the *something* had a name: idiopathic pulmonary fibrosis.

Idiopathic is a great word, isn't it? Kind of makes pulmonary fibrosis sound special, because it's not just pulmonary fibrosis. It's *idiopathic* pulmonary fibrosis.

The fact is, an idiopathic disease is a disease of an unknown cause. It's what the word actually means. IPF is a pulmonary disease (having to do with the lungs) where for unknown reasons (idiopathic) there is a progressive scarring of the lungs (fibrosis). So that's what I have—IPF. And while the cause is unknown, what we do know is this—it is incurable, it is progressive, and in some cases it is familial. That is, in some cases it can run in a family. It does in ours.

IPF took my father's life in 1999. It did the same to my oldest sister, Kathy, in 2018. My sister Cheri is presently, and bravely, navigating the latter stages of this disease. Now I know that I have it too.

A Tsunami of Stifled Grief

John: I was on my way home from meetings in downtown Minneapolis. Several new business opportunities were emerging, and I was delighted. It felt so good that all the hard work was paying off, and I could feel a calm and rest settling over my spirit.

But ten minutes from home, it suddenly felt like a hot coal had landed in the center of my chest, a pain like nothing I'd experienced before. I could feel my blood pressure rising and the pounding of my heartbeat in my ears. The air was being sucked out of my lungs. I started to sweat. In December. In Minnesota. These disturbing sensations felt exactly like what my wife, a cardiac critical care nurse by background, often described as a heart attack.

So I did what any rational person would do—I pulled into a parking lot outside Cub Foods, our local grocery store, to check my blood pressure with their free cuff located in the lobby. Sure enough, my blood pressure was off the charts.

When I arrived home, I tried to sound calm as I asked my wife how late she thought our doctor's office might be open. Because of her training, and forty years of living with this doctor-averse guy, Carol doesn't take any of my health questions as casual or random. After I reluctantly described my symptoms, within minutes we were on our way to the closest emergency room.

The fifteen-minute ride felt like an hour. My mind was spinning. *What if I have a heart condition? What if it's worse—the Big C? Will I see my grandkids grow up? Will we be able to enjoy the next stage of our life that we were just beginning to plan together? Is this the beginning of what I've seen other people my age experience, where even if the wheels don't completely fall off the bus, they start to wobble?* I was flooded with questions. And fear. Intense fear.

Thankfully, after monitoring, poking, prodding, and a full spectrum of cardiac tests and screens, the diagnosis was no heart attack or even cardiac irregularity. What had happened was a year's worth of bottled-up grief finally found its way to the surface, right in the center of my chest. I hadn't even been aware of the buried sorrow that refused to lie dormant. Our bodies don't lie.

Carol and I had suffered the loss of all three of our remaining parents in seven months, preceded by the deaths of a friend and the son of another good friend, intersected by the death of my favorite cousin, and followed by the death of a sister-in-law. Seven deaths. All in seven months. A tsunami of stifled grief had crashed over the shore of my life.

When Jesus said, "Blessed are those who mourn," He wasn't declaring, "Blessed are the bummed." He was stating that we are blessed when we get our deep interior sadness out to our exterior— when we quit pretending things are good when they are not. Only then can we find comfort. I hadn't been pretending. I simply wasn't paying attention to the true state of my soul. I had just kept on going . . . until I truly couldn't.

My body had made the choice for me to get my deep interior grief out. I didn't feel particularly "blessed" in that moment. I was overwhelmed. I felt like I was gasping for breath!

Breath-Obsessed People

When the idea for this book first came up, John and I weren't talking about my IPF or his grief. We were talking about what it takes to endure, to work through, to stay *in* something for the long haul. We were talking about life, and leadership, and faith, and hope, and how do you hang on to that . . . for the long haul?

Have you ever *lost* that? And if you have, how do you *recover* it?

Have you ever lost your breath? We both have, several times, and in different ways. And we both encounter many other leaders who are oxygen-depleted as well. Some are asphyxiated and don't even know it, because they haven't stopped long enough to catch their breath.

We also know young moms who are so out of breath from balancing their jobs with the care of children that they don't think they can go on. There are middle-aged men who've hit the wall in their work marathon and can't take the pressure of working another day in a job they've

Have you ever lost your breath?

always hated. We encounter seniors whose deteriorating health has them sharing a small room in a sterile care center with a roommate who watches the television all day, every day, at volume twelve.

Then smack in the middle of our writing, this book became

exponentially more relevant. The world is experiencing overlapping crises. We became a planet of breath-obsessed people.

A catastrophic pandemic, COVID-19, has as its primary symptom shortness of breath. Every country is impacted. The brokenness and fragility of our world was exposed. What were seemingly the foundations of security—wealth, relationships, religion, work, education, possessions—all have been swiftly, and in some cases permanently, shattered in a matter of months. Millions of people out of work. Businesses shuttered. Half the world's population confined to their homes. Trillions of dollars drained from the economy. Countless people infected with the virus. Over a million people breathing their last. All the uncertainty is leaving the world overwhelmed and gasping for breath. Anguish has replaced arrogance. We are experiencing a global hypoxia.

Even before the carnage of the coronavirus epidemic began to clear, all hell broke loose. The world was outraged to watch one man kneel for almost nine minutes on the neck of another man, squeezing out the last of his life as he pleaded, "I can't breathe!" That event triggered months of peaceful protests, spasms of violent rioting, looting, and mayhem, and deep reflection on centuries of simmering racial strife.

Has there ever been a more important time to examine how to recover your breath?

In It for the Long Haul

Annie Dillard submits, "Write as if you were dying. At the same time, assume you write for an audience consisting solely of terminal patients. That is, after all, the case. What would you begin writing if you knew you would die soon? What would you say to a dying person that would not enrage by its triviality?"[1]

This is far from trivial for either of us. Dave and I write with the urgency of dying men writing to dying readers! Dave has the painful physical reality of his IPF. I've held the hand of dying parents and thought I was on the threshold of heaven myself. None of us gets out of here alive. We are all terminally ill and on the clock. Most of us just don't have an expressed timetable.

I encounter business leaders regularly who are gasping for breath, literally or figuratively, in a business world that is convulsing with change and fueled by 24/7/365 demands aided and abetted by technology.

My grief took my breath away. I encounter business leaders regularly who are gasping for breath, literally or figuratively, in a business world that is convulsing with change and fueled by 24/7/365 demands aided and abetted by technology.

Dave couldn't breathe when he personally hit the wall at the ripe old age of thirty-nine. At the peak of what looked like tremendous pastoral success, he found himself exhausted, entirely spent, having nothing left to give his congregation. The road to recovery was not easy or quick, but having gone through it, he's sought out now by pastors and leaders who desperately want to stay in it for the long haul. They're willing to face the challenges of leading a meaningful ministry or a successful career *and* having a healthy life.

We're calling it *Gasping for Breath* because in one way or another, at one time or another, we all come up gasping for breath. In the athletic arena it's called "sucking air," when you have nothing left. Vince

Lombardi, the legendary coach for the Green Bay Packers, once said that "fatigue makes cowards of us all," because when you're tired you want to give up or give in. Maybe you're there right now in your work, faith, marriage, or ministry.

But don't give in. Just don't. Stay at it! Don't stop! Keep in it!

But what if you can't breathe? What if you *really* can't breathe?

This is why we wrote this book. We are talking about more than the exchange of air or the acquisition of oxygen. We're talking about the answer—inviting in the life-giving breath of God's Spirit and being *fully alive,* able to stay in it for the *long haul.*

Our Disclaimer

Here's our disclaimer: We are not candlelighters by nature. By candlelighters, we mean our deeply respected friends who get up early every morning, light a candle, spend hours silently reading Scripture, meditating on the profound meaning revealed in their time of solitude, journaling their innermost thoughts and insights, and then set off calmly and confidently into their day. That wasn't us, and we suspect it might not be you either.

For the longest time we both viewed the spiritual practices as being kind of soft . . . too "woo woo." We didn't say that out loud, but we thought it. However, we've discovered the hard way that they aren't soft. In fact, the "soft stuff" is the "hard stuff." Healthy rhythms of spiritual practice are essential, especially for Type A, ADHD, fidgety sorts like the two of us. We've both come to deeply understand, out of experiences that left us professionally, personally, and spiritually out of breath, how we've needed to learn and practice these disciplines. We're still learning and practicing. We'll try to unpack the why and the how of this in accessible and practical ways, backed up by Scripture, and narrated by stories of other real women and men.

Cynthia Bourgeault stated, "Virtually all spiritual paths begin their training with breath and tone—conscious breathing, following the breath, vibrating the mantra—and for good reason: these are actual tools and technologies for engaging and energizing our more subtle inner being."[2]

If any of this hits home, this book is for you. We will take a serious (and lighthearted), sacred (and secular), personal (and *sometimes* professional) look at how you can invite God's Spirit into your life, leadership, relationships, and faith when everything seems as though it is conspiring to suck the air right out of you.

READ—REFLECT—RESPOND

Pastor and author Mark Batterson has written: "Reading without meditating is like eating without digesting."[3] One approach to "eating this book" is to treat the READ—REFLECT—RESPOND exercises at the end of each chapter as a simple guide to deepening your individual faith journey by digesting each chapter on your own.

In his book *Celebration of Discipline*, Richard Foster says, "Books are best written in community."[4] This has certainly been true for us in writing *Gasping for Breath*. We have both grown personally and spiritually in the process.

Books are perhaps best read in community as well. The READ—REFLECT—RESPOND exercises provide a catalyst for deeper conversation and bolder action in pursuit of a Jesus-following life. They are intended to inspire small groups or learning communities to eat this book together rather than nibble on it alone.

You will be challenged to:

READ additional Scripture to enlarge your understanding of each topic covered.

REFLECT on questions to stimulate rich dialogue and deeper discovery.

RESPOND to a challenge intended to inspire bold action and catalyze a richer faith journey.

Take a deep breath, and let's get started together!

And the Lord God formed man from the dust of the earth

And He breathed into his nostrils the breath of life

And man became a living soul

Genesis 2

Just as breath, air, and wind is the very life of man,
so is the Spirit of God the life of the spiritual man.
By Him we are quickened at first; by Him we are kept
alive afterward; by Him the inner life is nurtured,
and increased, and perfected. The breath of the nostrils
of the man of God is the Spirit of God.

Charles Spurgeon

CHAPTER 1

First Breath

Our life begins and ends with breath.

Have you ever beheld a baby's first breath?

You'll never forget it. You know at your core that you just had a courtside seat at a miracle.

It sounds like a gasp, as the newborn's central nervous system reacts to the sudden change in temperature and environment, after having lived in the warmth of a total water world for nine months. The baby's lungs, which were filled with fluid during pregnancy, must suddenly fill with oxygen. Usually, within about ten seconds of birth, the respiratory center of the brain is jolted to tell the baby to take a breath . . . NOW!

It is the most profound change at birth—a baby's first breath. That first breath may also be the most difficult one the child takes until their last.

And have you ever held the hand of a friend or loved one as they breathed their last breath?

You'll never forget it. You know in your soul that you stood on the very threshold of sacred space.

That first breath begins a new story. And that last breath is in the words of C. S. Lewis for the children in the Chronicles of Narnia: "The beginning of the real story. All their life in this world and all their adventures . . . had only been the cover and the title page; now at last they were beginning Chapter One of the Great Story, which no one on earth has ever read; which goes on forever; in which every chapter is better than the one before."[5]

We all love a good story. And the great ones, the truly epic ones, often share similar themes. Universal themes of good and evil, life and death, love and loss, that when told really well can touch and unlock things in us that few other things can, because they're universal.

There you are crying at the end of a movie, hoping the lights don't go up because they got you again. They got you with that thing they do to make people cry, and right on cue—boom—there you are. I hate it when they do that, but I love it when they do that, because it's what good stories do—they move us. They make us laugh and make us cry. They lift our spirit and break our heart. They make us think. They help us feel. They quicken our pulse and animate our imagination. We are not passive bystanders in a great story. We are transported to different worlds, even to *galaxies far, far away.*

It's a story that began in eternity past, as wide as the universe, as old as forever. It's the story of God, and it began with a whisper. It began with breath.

But even if the story isn't real, if it didn't *really* happen—because Luke Skywalker wasn't *really* Darth Vader's estranged son, and four little hobbits weren't *really* on a quest to save Middle Earth—there's something imbedded in the story that is *true.* Universally true. Eternally true.

The irony in all of that is what makes those epic stories so effective. All of them are echoes of a much bigger story. It's a story that began in eternity past, as wide as the universe, as old as forever. It's the story of God, and it began with a whisper. It began with *breath*.

First Breath: The Breath of God

The ancient story begins with the swirling imagery of dust and earth and breath and life, the forming of man, and the breathing of the Lord God—*and He breathed into his nostrils the breath of life. And man became . . . alive . . . a living soul* (Genesis 2:7).

It all began in the beginning with this breath—the first breath. John and I thought we should write about this first, because long before we human beings began gasping for breath, there was *this* breath. It was the breath of God. It was the breath of life. When God breathed into the nostrils of this dust that had been formed into man, he became alive. But not just physically alive, he became spiritually alive—he became a *living soul*.

The imagery is vivid, and by it we're invited to imagine, and hopefully to see . . . *more*. More than oxygen filling the lungs, and more than dust becoming animated tissue. More than physically alive, like the birds of the air and the beasts of the field are alive, humankind became *more*. More than a mixture of oxygen, hydrogen, carbon, azote, and the ten other simple elements that comprise the totality of material existence and physical life.

It was more than physical breath that was breathed into man's nostrils, it was the breath of God, and he became *more*. More than the animated tissues of a living body, he became a living soul.

What If It's True?

What if more than a physical existence, we have a spiritual existence, an eternal existence? What if it's true? What if it really exists? More than a physical life, what if we actually have a spiritual dimension to our life? What if we have a *spiritual life*?

From time to time we might hear someone say, "I'm not very spiritual." I know what they mean, but what if it doesn't matter if they *think* they're not "very spiritual"? What if they have a spiritual life, whether they acknowledge it or not? What if?

What if you could separate the two and actually look at them? Your physical existence, over here; your spiritual existence, over there. I know, this is weird, but just go with us for a second.

What if when you come home from work today, you park your car in the garage and leave the window cracked so your spiritual existence can breathe, and you only bring your physical existence into the house? Try it. See how it works. Is this even possible?

The physical existence part is easy. I don't need my imagination to see it, because there it is staring back at me in the mirror. I can see it, feel it, and weigh it. I get hungry and thirsty. I get sleepy and tired. Sometimes I get sick, and someday I will physically die.

I have a heightened awareness of this physical existence with my IPF. John was suddenly tuned into this when he thought he was having a heart attack.

Seeing More

But if it's true that we're *more* . . .

If we're more than physically existing, can we be more than

physically hungry? Can we be *spiritually* hungry? And if we can, what do you feed a hungry spirit? What kind of food is good for the soul? What is spiritual junk food?

What kind of air does the human soul breathe? Is some air toxic for the soul? What about the lies we believe? Can lies about who we are, and who God is, and how life works be toxic to the soul, like polluted air?

If we're more than physically existing, can we be more than physically sick? Can we be spiritually sick or sleepy, strong or weak, alive or dead?

If we're more than physically existing, can we be physically healthy and strong, but spiritually sick and weak? That's a weird picture—physically, a human specimen, but spiritually, anemic.

Can the opposite be true? Can we be physically weak, even sick, but be spiritually vibrant? Can we be even physically dead, but spiritually alive—eternally alive?

All of which gets me to wondering, what do I care more about—my physical existence or my spiritual existence? Which one gets more attention, better care, healthier food, cleaner air?

Is either one *gasping for breath* right now?

It all began in the beginning, when God breathed into man's nostrils the breath of life and he became . . . *more*. Humans were perfectly in sync—physically and spiritually.

So from the very beginning it's been all about the breath and learning how to breathe.

Losing Our Breath

In the beginning it was good. God says it was *very* good. Having been

25

filled with the breath of God, made in the image of God, and fully alive to God, the crown of His creation was now walking with God in the cool of the day, and the breathing was easy. Indeed, they didn't even have to think about it. It was kind of like, well . . . breathing.

We take from 10 to 20 breaths a minute, about 14,000 to 28,000 breaths a day. Who actually thinks about their breath? Adam and Eve didn't have to think about theirs, because they were totally in step with God. And being totally in sync with God was effortless.

But then the story took a dark and tragic turn with a slithering snake, a venomous lie, and a poisonous fruit that opened their eyes. When their eyes were opened, what they saw was sin and death, and what they felt was ashamed, so what they did was to hide, first from God and then from each other. For the very first time they felt despair.

Never before had a despairing thought even entered their minds, but now they would never be free from them. Thus the pursuit began to find something, anything, that might relieve their sense of loss, and in their pursuit they started losing their breath. What had once been so natural and easy became labored and forced, marked by starts and stops and gasping for breath. We've been gasping for breath ever since.

Pressing Pause to Learn the Language of Metaphor

"Dear Lord," the pastor began the church service with arms extended and a rapturous look on his upturned face, "without You, we are but dust . . ."

He would have continued, but at that moment a little girl leaned over to her mother and asked loudly enough in her little girl voice for all to hear, "Mommy, what's 'butt dust'?"

Church was pretty much over at that point.

To modern ears such as ours, the language of Scripture can often sound as strange as "butt dust." Written in Hebrew and Greek, more than two millennia ago, in the context of ancient cultures with which we have little in common, it's not always easy to understand.

But it's not as hard as we think, if we know how to think metaphorically, poetically, and symbolically. Indeed, the real language of Scripture isn't merely Hebrew and Greek, it's the language of metaphor, simile, and symbol. That's a language that transcends time and crosses culture, which is at least part of why the Scriptures still speak. Scripture says of itself that it is "alive and active" (Hebrews 4:12 NIV), still living and breathing. It's not just some dusty book on a shelf to be exposited by "experts."

When their eyes were opened, what they saw was sin and death, and what they felt was ashamed, so what they did was to hide, first from God and then from each other. For the very first time they felt despair.

But it's not just time and culture that the language of metaphor (figurative language) helps us transcend, it's the fact that we're talking about God. In talking about God, we're trying to describe the indescribable. Which is why, according to Richard Rohr, the founder of the Center for Action and Contemplation, "All language about God is necessarily . . . metaphorical. Words [metaphors] are never the thing itself; they can only point toward the thing."[6] It's the only language that gives us access to transcendent reality. It helps us describe the indescribable, but the metaphor is never the thing itself.

When Jesus, for example, was trying to describe the indescribable realities of God's kingdom, He often spoke in parables using similes and metaphors. When He said that the "kingdom of heaven is like a treasure hidden in a field," it's "like a pearl of great price," and it's "like a sower going out to sow," He's saying the kingdom of heaven is *like* those things; they aren't *literally* those things. But the parable is still *literally* true.

When Jesus spoke in parables, He wasn't just telling pithy stories. He was putting one thing alongside another for comparison or illustration. Even in the original telling of the stories, His closest followers' response was often, "Huh?" Even they didn't always get the symbolism, because Jesus was using metaphors to describe a kingdom beyond their realm of experience or understanding.

Missing the Point, Literally

Not long ago in the context of a class I was teaching, I offhandedly suggested that there might not have been an actual sower going out to sow, who then got the exact same results that the sower in Jesus' parable got. I then clarified that what Jesus was teaching in the parable was true and it was real. But it didn't have to literally happen for it to be literally true, because it's a metaphor.

A very dear lady, whom I truly adore, approached me after class, visibly distressed. She was seriously undone, at least for a while, that there might be stories in the Bible that didn't literally happen the way they're literally described, but they're still literally true. Then I pushed her further, because I really like her, suggesting that if her perception of what's literally true about these stories demands that it literally happened the way it's literally described, she might literally be missing the point. She didn't laugh . . . until later.

Richard Rohr laments the fact that "Religion knew the truth of metaphor and symbol for almost all of history until the past few hundred years, and especially until the wrongly named Enlightenment in the seventeenth and eighteenth centuries. Then we started confusing rational and provable with real."[7]

So when we read that the Lord God *breathed into man's nostrils the breath of life*, and he became a *living soul,* the ancient writer isn't trying to provide a literal depiction or a scientific explanation for creation. What makes the story so compelling is that it invites us into a much bigger world than what might be scientifically true.

These things are eternally true and authentically real. But accessing that kind of reality requires metaphor, and analogy, and poetry. It's mythic, it's expansive, it's imaginative, it's beautiful—and it's real!

More and More Breath

With that in mind, let's return to the beginning of the story, where the breathing was easy and the crown of God's creation walked with Him in the cool of the day, until the story took a dark and tragic turn that left them breathless—and we've been gasping for breath ever since.

But that's not the end of the story, because this is God's story, and central to the story of God is that He never gives up. He never stops breathing. His breath is still available, not only for creating life but for re-creating it, renewing it, and restoring it.

It's why even today whenever a "fresh wind" of God's Spirit begins to blow through a church, or a city, or a nation, it's called a "revival," for things are being revived. They're coming to life or coming back to life.

God didn't just create. He's still creating. God didn't just breathe. He is still breathing. Right here. Right now.

Hebrew Grammar Stuff

There's a fascinating way that this continuous action of God is imbedded in a "hidden in plain sight" way through the grammatical structure of the original Hebrew in Genesis 2:7. Hang in there with us here. Don't bail out over the mention of Hebrew grammar. This may not be your cup of tea, but we think it's worth the work to think this through with us.

In Genesis 2:7, where it says that God *formed* the man and then He *breathed* into him the breath of life, both of those words (*formed* and *breathed*) are grammatically imperfect verbs. Now that doesn't mean that they're pretty good, above average verbs, solid B+ verbs, just not perfect verbs—as if they'd misbehaved in some way. An imperfect verb is a verb that indicates *continual action* in past time and *into the future*.

What that *continual action* means is that the God who *formed* us in the *past* (eternity past) is *continuing* to form us in the *present*, and He will *continue* to form us into the *future*.

It also means that the God who *breathed His life* into His creation in the *past* (eternity past), *continues* to *breathe life* in the *present*, and will *continue breathing life* into the *future*.

How 'Bout Them Bones?

There's an amazing picture of this in Ezekiel 37, where God gave the prophet Ezekiel a vision of the spiritual condition of His people, and it wasn't good. Indeed, they were dead. What he saw in the vision was a valley full of bones, which means they're dead. Those bones were very dry, which means they'd been dead for a very long time. That speaks metaphorically to hopelessness, because they're not only dead, they're really dead—they're a long time dead!

Is there hope for this thing or situation that seems to be dead, and it seems to have been dead for a very long time?

Which gives rise to the question Ezekiel asks: "Can these bones live?" (v. 3 NIV). Can they come to life? Is there any hope? It may be a question you've asked in the past. It may be a question you're asking right now.

That's a great question, because it's a question we human beings have been asking for a very long time.

Is there hope for this thing or situation that seems to be dead, and it seems to have been dead for a very long time? Is there hope for my lack of hope? Or for my marriage, or for this person whom I love, or for the church, or for my seemingly dead-end job, or for the way things are in the world right now? Is there hope?

It's a question being asked by millions of people in the midst of a global pandemic: Is there hope?

"I Will Cause Breath to Enter"

And the Spirit of the Lord answered and said, "Speak to the bones." Actually, He said, "Prophesy over these bones and say to them, 'O dry bones, hear the word of the LORD'" (v. 4 NASB).

Speaking to dead bones would be a very strange thing to do literally. But I've been a preacher for many years, so I find that picture no stranger than other preachers all across the country, maybe even around the world, who preach to dead people every week. And they've been dead for a very long time, because all they ever got was some impotent religion, and they never got truly filled with God's breath.

As a keynote speaker and leadership consultant, John has had many occasions to address a "hostage crisis"—rooms filled with people mandated to be there. Physically alive, he thinks, but often emotionally dying or dead in their careers. Is there hope?

Here's the word the prophet is told to deliver: "Tell them that I, the Lord God, will cause breath to enter you that you may come to life. I will put sinews on you, make flesh to grow back on you, and cover you with skin" (think Steven Spielberg's *A.I. Artificial Intelligence* movie), "and I will put My breath in you that you may come alive. And then you will know (not because you heard it in a sermon or read it in a book, but because you were touched by Me) that I am the Lord your God" (vv. 5–6).

Get the picture?

Now fast forward to Acts 2, where on the day of Pentecost it happens again, because when the Spirit was poured out in verse 2, they heard a noise *like the sound of rushing wind*—it was the breath of God. Here He is again, in a very real sense, breathing on His people. He's filling them with His Spirit, with His breath, with His life, and 3,000 souls come to life (v. 41).

Fast forward again to Ephesians 2:5, where the apostle Paul, perhaps informed by the metaphors and imagery of Ezekiel's vision, says essentially that much like the dry bones of our ancestors, we were *dead* in our sins. That means we weren't just sinners who needed forgiveness, we were dead people who needed to somehow be *brought to life!*

God began to do in them what He's been doing from the very beginning, and what He did in Ezekiel's vision when He came with

His Breath Spirit, and what He did in His closest followers sheltering in place on Pentecost, and what He continues to do today. He came with His Spirit (He put it into them), and He came with His life and gave it to them, and they came to life!

All of which leads us to the BIG question in this first chapter . . .

Are You Saved?

When I was a kid, growing up the way I did in church, the big question was always this: Are you saved? Specifically, from hell. Are you going to go to heaven when you die? It was all about getting saved, trying to get people saved, and wondering if we were saved, because we didn't want to burn in hell. We wanted to go to heaven when we died.

My dad was the pastor of the church I grew up in. One Sunday morning when I was around ten years old, I was sitting in church, listening to my dad preach, and I got a bad case of the "squirmies." ADHD squirmy. Though I meant no disrespect to my dear departed dad (who was a heckuva preacher), I couldn't sit still.

But I survived that service, and after the final song had been sung and the final prayer had been prayed, as we all stood up to leave, the lady sitting in front of me—who in my memory still looks like the Wicked Witch of the West—turned around and asked me, in pretty much the same tone that the Wicked Witch asked Dorothy about her little dog, Toto, "Are you *SAVED*?"

Apparently, my squirming had so disturbed her worship experience that it caused her to question the condition of my soul, and even my eternal destiny. "Are you *SAVED*?"

Well, in that moment I wanted to be, I really did. But mostly from her!

Are You Alive?

Over the years that story has become funnier than it ever was disturbing, but I still can't help but notice that it helped create a shift in me with regard to the BIG question. Because while I still believe that "Are you saved?" is a good enough question, a far more compelling question, at least to me now, is this: "Are you ALIVE?" *Fully* ALIVE?

It all began in the beginning when God breathed the breath of life into man's nostrils, and he became a living soul. He was ALIVE.

But not just physically alive, he was made spiritually alive. More than a physical life, he has a spiritual life. More than a physical existence, he has a spiritual existence as well.

We're going to take a leap and assume if you are reading this book, you're physically alive to some extent. But are you *really* alive—physically *and* spiritually? Are you breathing easy, or are you gasping for breath?

And if you are alive, *why* are you alive? What are you here on earth to do?

Back from the Dead

For thirteen years, Garrett (not his real name) wasn't just gasping for breath, he was walking around dead. He wandered homeless, panhandled on street corners, and mugged strangers for money to buy his next crack fix. His drug and alcohol use accelerated from recreational to habitual after his older brother slammed into a parked dump truck at fifty miles per hour, shearing off the car's roof, and then his younger brother committed suicide.

Garrett descended into the cycle of treatment, halfway houses, and relapse. Every attempt to arrest his free fall back into drugs was met with self-inflicted failure. After more than a dozen treatment centers and countless homeless shelters, he had burned up the system, had nothing left to sell, and no one left to call.

When Garrett wandered shoeless into the Salvation Army building, he was greeted at the door with, "Welcome. We're so glad you're here!" That evening at chapel, one man put his arms around Garrett, looked directly into his eyes, and said, "I'm here to tell you that your nightmare is over."

Desperately needing that to be true, but not believing it possible, Garrett replied, "Look, buddy, this isn't my first rodeo. I've been in and out of treatment for years."

The man repeated, "You're not listening! I'm here to tell you that your nightmare is over. The horror story you've been living is over."

It was an Ezekiel 37 moment. New breath—God's Spirit—was breathed into Garrett.

Garrett was dead. Now he was coming alive, *fully alive.*

Few stories of life transformation are as dramatic. Few people are as desperate as Garrett was. But each of us longs for something more, something different. We have a deep desire to live a life of significance and meaning. A life where we're fully alive. A life where we're inhaling deeply the Breath that is in us from the very beginning. How do you get that life?

Sometimes we grow up only when it's the last available option. We have to hit the wall before we wake up to our own breathlessness.

That was true for both of us.

READ—REFLECT—RESPOND

Chapter One: First Breath

THEME: *God breathed life into you*

READ the following Scriptures:

- ☐ Genesis 1—2
- ☐ Ezekiel 37:1–14

REFLECT on the following questions:

- ☐ Can you identify a time when you experienced what you might call "the breath of God"?
- ☐ Are you ever aware of your own breathing? When? Why?
- ☐ We made a distinction between being "Saved" and being "Alive." Does that distinction make sense to you, or is it confusing? Why?
- ☐ If we're more than physically existing, can we be more than physically hungry? Can we be spiritually hungry? If we can, what kind of food do you feed a hungry soul?
- ☐ If we're more than physically existing, can we be more than physically sick? Can we be spiritually sick or sleepy, strong or weak, alive or dead?
- ☐ Between your physical existence and your spiritual existence, which gets more attention, better care, healthier food, cleaner air?

RESPOND to the following challenge:

Do an inventory of your physical and spiritual diet.

- ☐ Which one are you more careful about?
- ☐ What kind of junk food do you like?
- ☐ What kind of food do you eat most?
- ☐ What is the equivalent of a spiritual junk food, something with empty spiritual carbs?

*Come to me, all you who are weary and
burdened, and I will give you rest.*

Matthew 11

*There's freedom in hitting bottom . . .
relief in admitting you've reached the
place of great unknowing.*

Anne Lamott

Gasping for Breath

"John, what is your father like?"

It was a great question . . . but not at that moment. My father was in the last stages of dying from stage 4 bladder cancer. We had moved him into hospice the day before. He hadn't been conscious or responsive for two days.

After watching him closely, holding his hand, praying and singing over him, and whispering into his ear that it was "Okay to go," my mom and I decided to take a short break and grab a quick bite to eat before resuming our bedside vigil. When we returned an hour later, we noticed immediately that Dad's breathing pattern had changed dramatically. He was laboring and quietly moaning with each short breath. My mom stayed by his side as I raced down the hall to summon the night nurse.

When I described his symptoms to the nurse, she calmly informed me that he was experiencing "agonal breathing," which is the medical term used to describe struggling to breathe or gasping for breath. It is a symptom of a severe medical emergency, such as a stroke or cardiac arrest. It may also indicate, as in this case, that my dad was one step closer to dying.

I was anxious to get back to his side, but as the nurse slowly walked behind me to the room, she suddenly stopped, gestured toward a hallway bench, and said, "Sit with me for a minute."

I sat down beside her, dreading that she was about to describe the painful reality of my dad's last few hours. Instead, the compassionate, wise nurse gently asked, "John, what is your father like?"

I looked at her somewhat dumbfounded, thinking, *What an odd question. What difference does it make at this moment?*

However, she recognized that I was out of breath, partly from running to get her, and partly because I was so anxious in the surreal surrounding that I was neglecting to breathe myself. I had watched my father-in-law die two years previous, but somehow this was different. It was more personal. More painful. Especially sitting by my heartbroken mother's side. The nurse's seemingly ill-timed question was intended to calm me down. To remind me to inhale and exhale.

Breathe in. Breathe out. Repeat.

It worked. As I sat with her, I began to reminisce about times with my dad when I was growing up—family vacations, sports, funny sayings, quirky habits, lessons learned—all good things. My breathing slowly returned to a normal rhythm.

After a few minutes, she stood up and said, "Well, let's go see your dad."

Agonal Leading

I frequently encounter leaders who are experiencing a sort of agonal breathing in their work and life. They are honestly one step closer to dying—perhaps not physically, but emotionally, relationally, and spiritually. They just may not know it . . . yet.

Recently, one extraordinarily successful business leader quietly confessed as we were celebrating with his newly formed team at a lavish, multicourse dinner, "I would like nothing more than to be at home right now. I'm completely exhausted."

Another leader told me, "I have to muster all my energy to get on the train every morning to commute into the office."

And still another said, "The stress of this past year caused me to have one or two drinks with my husband at dinner, tuck the kids into bed, and then have another two to four drinks as I powered through hundreds of emails until well after midnight. The next day I would get up and do it all again, on four hours' sleep."

I used to get on the elevator in our office building surrounded by people who were living the seminal moment of the movie *The Sixth Sense* when nine-year-old Haley Joel Osment whispered, "I see dead people." Many of those office workers were walking, standing upright, but barely breathing. First thing Monday morning, they were desperate for Friday to come quickly.

When I'm speaking to groups, I occasionally jokingly ask them, "How many of you woke up this morning?" Not immediately catching the whole question, about a third of the participants raise their hands. As it begins to sink in, there's always a ripple of nervous laughter. They've caught themselves in the act of being themselves!

Then I ask, "How many of you set an alarm to wake up?" Usually the majority.

"How many of you hit snooze this morning?" Also, usually the majority.

"How many of you hit snooze twice?" A few hands go down.

"Three times?" A few more hands go down.

The most I've ever heard is eight times. Eight times! The person set the alarm for 4:00 a.m. to get up at 6:00 a.m. That is either a symptom of a *very* slow riser or a person who is out of breath in their life and/or work.

My follow-up question to them, and to you, is, "What is your first impulse when the alarm goes off?"

Do you feel *burned out*? Before your feet even hit the floor, are you gasping for breath, defeated by deadlines, and worn down by the worry of keeping all the balls in the air today? Are your family, fitness, finances, and faith running on fumes? Is your check engine light on?

Are you gasping for breath, defeated by deadlines, and worn down by the worry of keeping all the balls in the air today? Are your family, fitness, finances, and faith running on fumes? Is your check engine light on?

Or are you feeling *rusted out*? Are you holding your breath while you just mark time in your relationships, spiritual life, and work? Are you waiting for yet another season to pass, putting your life on hold, until "someday"—the weekend, a staycation, or retirement? Is your passion on pause? How long can you hold your breath?

I've been that person more than once. Rushing to get somewhere, not quite being anywhere. Trying to say yes way too often, while forgetting that NO can be a complete sentence.

Refusing to Rest

There is a hauntingly clear picture of this when God, the Sovereign Lord, the Holy One of Israel, says this to His people through the prophet Isaiah:

In returning and rest, you will be saved. In quietness and trust you will find strength. But you refused. *You couldn't sit still;* instead, you said, "No! We will ride out of here on horseback. Fast horses will give us an edge in battle."

But those who pursue you will be faster still. When one person threatens, a thousand will panic and flee. When five terrorize you, all will run pell-mell, until you are as conspicuous as a single flag standing high on a hill.

Meanwhile, the Eternal One yearns to give you grace and boundless compassion; that's why He waits. For the Eternal is a God of justice. Those inclined toward Him, waiting for His help, will find happiness.

Isaiah 30:15–18 THE VOICE

Here's what we wonder. Is it possible to be that person—*fleeing on horses and refusing to rest*—yet not even be aware that that's what you're doing? To not be aware that you're saying to God, "I don't need You for this task. I have a fast horse and boatloads of talent, and energy too." To not be aware that you're saying to God, "I don't really believe that in quietness and trust I'll find the strength I need. I already have the strength I need, and, oh, by the way, I have a really fast horse."

So we run, and we run, and we run.

And He waits.

Like a Flag on a Hill

John and I both have tried to outrun the burnout and the rust out . . . to no avail. At the age of thirty-nine, and twelve years into a career that was by all accounts successful, I hit the wall. Physically and emotionally spent, I found myself in a place of exhaustion from which I couldn't recover—at least not quickly. People around me seemed to realize it before I did, that I wasn't just out of *gas*, I was out of *oil*. And if I didn't find a way to shut my engine down, I'd likely do permanent damage to myself.

But how do you do *that*? Who *gets* to do that? There's too much to do, right? You have to keep going and find a really fast horse.

My career was not in the context of business or industry, and I wasn't the CEO of a large corporation. I was the senior pastor of a rapidly growing church, and while the leadership demands of the corporate and religious worlds might appear to be quite different, both come with complexities and pressures that can be difficult to manage.

I came to pastor the Church of the Open Door in 1980 as a twenty-seven-year-old kid with a whole lot of energy and a ton of passion. Wisdom, however, takes time. That would come later, accompanied by layers of scar tissue.

The growth of the church was slow at first, as the culture needed to change, but when it did, the growth was explosive. Our church of 160 people swelled to somewhere near 5,000 in just a few years. It was heady stuff to be told by people who keep track of these things that we were among the ten fastest-growing churches in America. We were even given a plaque to prove it!

But while the growth was exciting, and the ministry was making a significant impact, twelve years of an ever-increasing pace took its toll on me. The symptoms were subtle at first, and easy to ignore. So I did.

Indeed, I did what we all try to do—just power through. You keep *going*, but you also keep *ignoring*, and you also keep *believing* that if you could just fix *this*, and maybe tweak *that,* you'd finally be able to breathe again.

Hitting the wall is when you realize that you can't. It's when you realize that regardless of how hard you try or how fast you move to keep all the plates spinning, you just can't, and they all come crashing down.

> *Hitting the wall is when you realize that regardless of how hard you try or how fast you move to keep all the plates spinning, you just can't, and they all come crashing down.*

Author and speaker Anne Lamott says about it, "There's freedom in hitting bottom, in seeing that you won't be able to save or rescue your daughter, her spouse, his parents, or your career, relief in admitting you've reached the place of great unknowing. This is where restoration can begin, because when you're still in the state of trying to fix the unfixable, everything bad is engaged: the chatter of your mind, the tension of your physiology, all the trunks and wheel-ons you carry from the past. It's exhausting, crazy-making."[8]

Early on, I thought a vacation could fix it. I just needed some time off, so I took some days right after Christmas. We didn't want to travel, so we did a staycation. We watched movies, ate pizza, played games with the kids, and relaxed—it was great! But on Thursday of that week, my wife made this observation: "Dave, you're a grump! Here we are on vacation, but you're still all amped up, you're short with the kids, you act like you're angry, and I don't think you notice."

But I *had.* I just didn't think *she* had. Which meant I was busted!

So maybe it was time to look closer at this thing called "my life." Because what dawned on me that week was that when I slowed down, even a little, I started to actually *feel* the things I couldn't feel while I kept going frenetically. It wasn't until I stopped for a staycation, for just a few days, that I finally felt how exhausted I was. And resentful. Maybe that's what the anger was about. I was afraid that if I slowed down, I'd fall behind. I wouldn't keep up.

I didn't dare sit still. I'd be like a flag flapping on a hill. Alone. I had to keep going and find a faster horse.

The Sabbatical from Hell

I hung on until late March, when the assessment of the elders—that I wasn't just out of gas, I was out of oil—resulted in a decision for me to take a sabbatical.

A sabbatical! How exotic! Just in the nick of time, and just what I needed. Some room to breathe. I think I'm going to be fine.

The only problem was, I had no idea what I was supposed to do. What do people do on sabbaticals? I knew immediately that the picture I'd developed of sitting by a stream under a tree, slowly chewing on a blade of grass while thinking deep thoughts, was probably not going to happen. What *did* happen, however, was not part of any picture I imagined.

It ultimately became known by everyone who knew us as the sabbatical from hell. I'm not kidding!

First, Bonnie and I joined a coed softball team, thinking that was a very "sabbatical kind of thing to do." We had no sense of lurking danger. Indeed, it felt great to be starting this time off with an activity that we both enjoyed, that we could do together, and that we normally wouldn't do, because we *normally* wouldn't have time for such a thing.

I can still see it in my mind's eye. In her very first at bat, Bonnie hit a line drive over the shortstop's head into left-center field, knocking in two runs. But with that one swing of the bat—something that most people are able to walk away from unscathed—she blew out her knee, broke her ankle in three places, and our season was over!

A week later, at the pre-op exam for the surgery on her knee, the doctors found a lump on her throat. The discussion suddenly shifted to cancer, so the knee would have to wait. The good news was that the surgery on her throat went well. It wasn't cancer, and we were all relieved, at least for a while.

Next, on a hot summer day in early July, a thunderstorm came roaring through our neighborhood. Like most summer storms, it was violent and brief, but it stayed long enough to strike a few homes in the area with lightning. Ours was one of them. The lightning started a fire, which gutted our house. Just like that, we lost our home.

Fortunately, we have friends. We are part of a church community that loves us, and people's generosity toward us was stunning as we never lacked a place to stay for the next three months. It helped that it was summer, because people would leave town on vacation and often offer us their home while they were gone. That part was amazing!

But then it started getting funny. Not ha ha funny. More like "What the heck is going on here?" funny. Inexplicably, in every place we stayed, every home that had been opened to us—I'm not making this up—we broke something significant. And expensive! Like the $300 fishing pole that snapped in half when our son Caleb pushed it a little beyond its limit. I didn't know that fishing poles can cost $300, or that you can snap them in half as easily as he did. But they do. And he did.

It actually became absurd when I walked into the garage of a house where we'd been staying and noticed that a tire on the car the owners had left for us had gone flat. All by itself. It just went flat. We had to laugh, but it wasn't a ha ha laugh; it was a . . . well, you know.

But the hardest thing in all of this was that I still couldn't breathe. In part because I couldn't rest. I just didn't know how. Being given time off had been a wonderful gift, but I realized I needed more than a stoppage of work to recover my breath. This would take some time.

Ultimately, with the help of some friends, a very patient wife, and a couple of really good counselors, I started to come back to life. (More on this in Chapter 5.) And while the road to recovery was not a short one, it was ultimately a good one. In part because I realized I needed more than some rest and a little time off. I needed to recalibrate. I needed to examine those things that had been unexamined, particularly those things in my soul.

Though parts of the process were painful, it marked the beginning of a journey that was driven by this question: How do you stay in it for the long haul?

But by *it*, I don't mean the *ministry*—you don't need to be in ministry to serve the purposes of God. I mean the *faith*. And by *faith*, I don't mean *orthodoxy*, as if believing the right things about God is what will keep us safe.

How do you stay in it for the long haul?

I mean being a person who is *full of faith*, and *hope*, and *confidence* in God, regardless of how our ministry or work is going, or how successful we might be.

A Common Leadership Malady

If you think Dave's experience is unique, think again. (Well, actually, blowing out a knee, breaking an ankle, burning down a house, snapping a $300 fishing pole, and randomly finding a flat tire on a car—all on one sabbatical—is unique.) But being a breathless leader is more common than we'd like to admit. We've all gasped for breath at one time or another.

According to research from the Barna Group, a Christian polling firm:

> More than a third of pastors are at a high or medium risk of burnout, and three quarters know at least one fellow pastor whose ministry ended due to stress. Nearly half of pastors are at a high or medium relational risk, whether they are experiencing challenges in marriage, family, friendships, or other close relationships. And, one in five pastors has struggled with an addiction—most commonly to porn—while almost half have faced depression.[9]

However, sucking air in one's calling or work is not restricted to ministry leaders. Jim Harter, a chief scientist at Gallup Research, states:

> The percentage of "engaged" workers in the U.S.—those who are involved in, enthusiastic about, and committed to their work and workplace—is now 34 percent. The percentage who are "actively disengaged"—workers who have miserable work experiences—is now 13 percent. The remaining 53 percent of workers are in the "not engaged" category. They may be generally satisfied but are not cognitively and emotionally connected to their work; they will usually show up to work and do the minimum

required but will quickly leave their company for a slightly better offer.[10]

Harter adds that leadership accounts for at least 70 percent of the variance in worker engagement.

Healthy leader—healthy church or business. Unhealthy leader—sick church or business.

You are not designed to live this way! How do you get more air into your lungs?

Let's go back to the hospice nurse's incisive question.

What Is Your Father Like?

Are you like author Brennan Manning, who for a long time saw God the Father as "a small-minded bookkeeper, a niggling customs officer rifling through our moral suitcase, as a policeman with a club who is going to bat us over the head every time we stumble and fall, or as a whimsical, capricious, and cantankerous thief who delights in raining on our parade and stealing our joy"[11]?

Or do you perhaps envision God as writer Philip Yancey did, who "grew up with the image of a mathematical God, who weighed my good and bad deeds on a set of scales and always found me wanting—a distant and thundering figure who preferred fear and respect to love"[12]?

If we view God in these ways, we are likely to exhaust ourselves trying to please Him or everybody else. We will end up out of breath—worn out, weary, burdened, bitter—and give up.

Or as Dave did, you'll come to unknowingly believe the lie that you can't live a well-rounded, God-honoring life *and* be a successful leader. There may be a smoldering discontent that eventually ignites into full-fledged anger that no amount of staycations will extinguish. It will literally suck the life and breath right out of your lungs and soul.

So how do you begin to take deep breaths again?

Jesus, who was perfectly in step with His Father while on earth, gives us the key to a well-lived life:

> "Come to me, all you who are weary and burdened,
> and I will give you rest. Take my *yoke* upon you and
> learn from me, for I am gentle and humble in heart,
> and you will find rest for your souls. For my *yoke* is
> easy and my burden is light."
> Matthew 11:28–30 NIV

For non-farmers like us, when Jesus refers to a *yoke*, we can read it figuratively or literally. An ox yoke in Jesus' time was made of wood. Oxen were brought in, measured, and a yoke was custom made to fit, so it wouldn't wear a bloody sore into the neck of the animal as it went about its work. Jesus, the carpenter, likely knew a thing or two about fashioning and custom fitting wooden ox yokes. Likewise, God our Father certainly knows a thing or two about fashioning and custom fitting the yoke of our capacity and giftedness, so we don't wear ourselves out as we go about the work of our lives.

Every rabbi in Jesus' day also had his own interpretation of the Torah, the law of God as revealed to Moses and recorded in the first five books of the Hebrew Bible, called his *yoke*. When you followed a rabbi, you placed yourself in the yoke of that rabbi. Unfortunately, most religious teachers then and now succumb to the gravitational pull of adding to the words of Scripture through their personal interpretations.

Maybe it's ego. Maybe it's the desire to demonstrate importance, relevance, or to build out one's "unique value proposition." But the universal tendency is to complexify and multiply rather than simplify matters of faith, life, and business.

Religions tend to add rules and regulations. In Jesus' time, the Pharisees had added 600-plus specific rules for following the Sabbath, thus perfecting the art of making rest impossibly exhausting.

Similarly, today's businesses build out "leadership competencies," and then try to force fit people into an onerous list of "have to have" attributes, skills, and experiences that no mere mortal possesses. It's all so tiring!

Do you want to learn to live freely and lightly? Are you ready to learn and live the unforced rhythms of grace?

A small group of leaders who were intending to launch a leadership institute for pastors once visited our leadership consultancy office. They had landed on the idea that the curriculum should be organized around fifty-plus leadership competencies that they believed all pastors needed to possess in order to be an effective ministry leader. At the conclusion of their pitch to us, I suggested tongue-in-cheek that we weren't the right firm to help build and lead the institute because "I doubted that Jesus Himself had all fifty." Once the shock wore off them, we discussed how to architect a curriculum around leadership strengths and spiritual gifts, and then to delegate the rest to other members of the church body, who would be energized to serve from their giftedness.

We like how *The Message* states Jesus' words from Matthew 11:28–30 that we quoted previously. Jesus asks, "Are you tired? Worn out? Burned out on religion?" Here's His practical, but by no means easy, solution:

> "Come to me. Get away with me and you'll recover your life. I'll show you how to take a real rest. Walk with me and work with me—watch how I do it. Learn the unforced rhythms of grace. I won't lay anything heavy or ill-fitting on you. Keep company with me and you'll learn to live freely and lightly."

Do you want to learn to live freely and lightly? Are you ready to learn and live the unforced rhythms of grace?

Are you longing to get off your fast horse and join the One who has been waiting for you all along?

We did too. But before we could breathe easy, however, we both had to acknowledge some of the toxic air we were breathing in and the bad breath we were breathing out.

READ—REFLECT—RESPOND

Chapter Two: Gasping for Breath

THEME: *We've all gasped for breath*

READ the following Scriptures:

- ☐ Isaiah 30:15–18
- ☐ Matthew 11:25–30

REFLECT on the following questions:

- ☐ What's *your* story? When have you found yourself gasping for breath?
- ☐ What kind of thing most often takes your breath away? What takes your breath away the quickest?
- ☐ What is your first impulse when the alarm goes off in the morning?
- ☐ Does God help you catch your breath, or is how you see Him part of the problem?
- ☐ What is your view of the Father?

RESPOND to the following challenge:

- ☐ Tell someone you trust about your breathing. Are you gasping for breath?

I heard the sound of You in the garden, and I was afraid because I was naked; so I hid myself.

Genesis 3

On the surface of our lives, most of us build the hard shell. It is built to cover fear and insecurity and win approval and success.

David Brooks

CHAPTER 3

Bad Breath

In my book *Dare to Answer: 8 Questions That Awaken Your Faith*, I tell the story of my friend Tom who carried two business cards.[13] One card with his real name was for his successful consulting practice. The second card with a pseudonym was for his avocation of creating a remarkable photo narrative titled "Shadow Man" that featured images of his shadow set in a wide variety of natural and manufactured backdrops. Tom's fear was that his gift of photographic artistry would somehow be diminished by his everyday identity of accountant, consultant, and CEO. Conversely, he worried that no one would take him seriously as a consultant if they knew he was out taking photos of his shadow next to cacti and street signs.

Here's the question: Are you a shadow man or woman?

Richard Rohr defines your shadow as, "What you refuse to see about yourself, and what you do not want others to see."[14] Are you hiding behind your own shadow? Or something else?

In his book *Backpacking with the Saints*, Belden Lane asks, "What happens when a 'gifted child' finds himself in a wilderness where he's stripped of any way of proving his worth? What does he do when there's nothing he can do, when there's no audience to applaud his performance, when he faces a cold, silent indifference, if not hostility? His world falls to pieces. The soul hungry for approval starves in a desert like that."[15]

Such is the plight of our false self, when the strategies that helped it survive and even thrive early in life are painfully exposed as being an inadequate source of protection. They worked for a while, and in truth they were all that you had. But when you're forty, the fact that you were the class clown or the overachiever in high school doesn't cut it anymore. When that day comes, you won't be able to breathe.

It all began in the beginning, when Adam said to God, "I heard the sound of You in the garden, and I was afraid because I was naked; so I hid myself" (Genesis 3:10 NASB).

And we've been hiding ever since!

Naked and Not Ashamed

This was never the desire of God, and certainly not the design for His creation in the beginning. There was no reason to hide. Indeed, as the story is told through the Holy Spirit-guided writers, they visualize a time before shame and fear when the crown of His creation, both male and female, walked with God in the cool of the day and the breathing was easy. They were both naked and not ashamed (Genesis 2:25).

One day when we went to visit our kids and grandkids, the door of their house swung wide open and we were greeted by our three-year-old grandson standing joyfully buck naked! He couldn't have cared less by the surprised look on our faces. He had absolutely no shame. That was Adam and Eve in the garden.

But it's not just physical nakedness that this Eden depicts; it's beyond the embarrassment (or shame) one might feel if physically exposed that's in view. The nakedness without shame in Genesis 2 is the nakedness of full disclosure. Not just your body, but *you*. All of *who you are*, exposed—but without any shame. They were entirely unguarded (they were naked) with nothing to fear (they were naked but not ashamed), so there was nothing to hide and no need to conceal anything from God or from each other. As David Brooks, the op-ed columnist for the *New York Times*, states, there was no need, for the "hard shell" we build "to cover our fear and insecurity and win approval and success."[16]

Can you even imagine such a thing? To be entirely unguarded with nothing to fear. Can you imagine that?

How about with your spouse, or with that person you call your best friend, or with the people in your small group at church? How about the guys you smoke cigars with on Tuesday night, or the people you work with, or the people you work for? Is there anyone, anywhere, with whom you can be entirely unguarded? Naked and unashamed?

Can you even imagine such a thing? To be entirely unguarded with nothing to fear.

Well, the idyllic existence of Genesis 2 didn't last long. In Genesis 3, the unguarded vulnerability of this Eden came to a screeching halt when we read that "their eyes were opened, and they saw that they were naked." But this time, they were ashamed.

Immediately, they did what we all do when we're naked and ashamed—we cover up and we conceal. Instead of breathing easy as they walked with God in the cool of the day, the man and his wife "hid themselves from the presence of the Lord God" (Genesis 3:8 NASB).

They hid themselves, but not before "they sewed fig leaves together and made coverings for themselves" (v. 7 NIV).

It's Just the Way It Is

Now this instinct we have to cover up and conceal those things we don't want anyone to see about our actual selves is just part of the human condition. Particularly if that includes any weakness or fear or maybe failure.

We sew fig leaves together—not to deceive or hurt anyone else, but to protect ourselves. We sew together a polished persona, a certain face, an impressive résumé, and put it on, and only when we're fully clothed can we go outside.

It began in the beginning, and we've been doing it ever since. In fact, we've gotten really good at this, and our fig leaves have grown more elaborate and much more refined. They're more attractive, and sometimes they're quite convincing. John Eldredge observes we're so good at it that "most of what you encounter when you meet a man is a façade, an elaborate fig leaf, a brilliant disguise."[17]

I used to meet periodically with a friend who, at that time, was the CEO of a multibillion-dollar corporation with hundreds of thousands of employees. Even though we were friends, and the purpose of our meeting was simply to have a cup of coffee and catch up, he would be guarded and cautiously scripted for the first fifteen minutes, speaking in cryptic business jargon. I was having a business-only conversation with his fig leaf!

Finally, when it clicked that this wasn't an analyst call and that whatever he said wasn't going any further than where we were sitting, he would relax and become himself—just my friend. He would step out from behind his fig leaf and become real. His role required that he adopt a certain kind of persona (fig leaf) for the stockholders, employees, and general public, and a quite different (real) identity for family and friends.

We all have numerous roles we play, whether as spouse, parent, grandparent, employee, partner, leader, pastor, or volunteer. The question is, do these different roles also come equipped with different identities? Is one a shadow man or woman? Are some true and others a fig leaf? Or are you the real you in all the different roles, albeit with some different norms, behaviors, and responsibilities?

Psychologist David Benner warns, "While this might seem quite benign, the dark side is that what begins as a role becomes an identity. Initially the masks we adopt reflect how we want others to see us. Over time, however, they come to reflect how we want to see our self."[18] It isn't so much an evil thing, in the way we think of evil, but it certainly is false. It's a false self.

All of us do this to one degree or another, in part because it's easy to do, and we feel pressure to do it, so it just becomes the mask we wear and the image we've created. Some people call it the impostor, and sometimes it shows up as a poser. Posers are usually easy to spot, and easy to make fun of, but the impostor can be pretty slick. Sometimes we can't spot that one, even in ourselves.

Thomas Merton says it this way: "Every one of us is shadowed by an illusory person: a false self. This is the [person] that I want myself to be but who cannot exist, because God does not know anything about him. And to be unknown of God is altogether too much privacy. My false and private self is the one who wants to exist outside the reach of God's will and God's love—outside of reality and outside of life. And such a self cannot help but be an illusion. We are not very good at recognizing illusions, least of all the ones we cherish about ourselves."[19]

Form and Essence

Everything has both *form* and *essence*. *Form* is what you see on the outside. It is the appearance of something. For instance, a marriage, business, church, parent, and leader all have a certain *form*. It can be things such as timeliness, communication ability, physical appearance, worship style, behaviors, and practices, even signs of affection.

What if our form doesn't line up with our essence?

Form is how we quickly fashion first impressions of others. In an increasingly social media-driven world where we develop opinions based on sound bites, Instagram, and TikTok clips, *form* is becoming increasingly (and tragically) more important. We can end up spending a lot of time—a lifetime, in fact—fabricating a really beautiful *form*.

Essence is what is truly inside a person, relationship, church, or business. It consists of values, giftedness, a sense of purpose and calling and vision. Essence is who we *truly* are.

What if our *form* doesn't line up with our *essence*? The *form* of a family, for example, may appear to be the Instagram-curated, perfect life of a happy, always loving, and in sync marriage. Photos show *Travel & Leisure* worthy vacations, a perfectly groomed and well-behaved golden retriever, a Pinterest designed house, and 4.5 GPA Mensa-smart kids in preschool. You know, like what you see in every Christmas letter you receive! "That family."

But what if that *form* is really an elaborate fig leaf, covering up something quite different? What if the truth is the version that plays out in the car on the way to church right up to the second they hop out and put on the "perfect family smiley face for the churchy friends" *essence*? What you're seeing is really an elaborate illusion—a tailored tuxedo or beautiful floor-length cocktail dress sewn of fig leaves.

David Benner says about it: "Because it is hollow at the core [essence], the life of a false self is a life of excessive attachments. Seeking to avoid implosion and nonbeing, the false self grasps for anything [form] that appears to have substance and then clings to these things with the tenacity of a drowning man clutching a life ring."[20]

Thomas Merton describes it as only he can: "But there is no substance under the things with which I am clothed. I am hollow, and my structure of pleasures and ambitions has no foundation. . . . And when they are gone there will be nothing left of me but my own nakedness and emptiness and hollowness, to tell me that I am my own mistake."[21]

Fig Leaves and Football

I (Dave) was a sixteen-year-old high school kid when I got my first real fig leaf. It's not that I was consciously aware of my "false-self strategies and the core beliefs that drive them," because that's not the kind of language I would use or understand. But I was developing a false-self strategy nonetheless. Growing up on the South Side of Chicago, I was looking for the fig leaf that might fit me. Turns out, we start doing that pretty early.

My mom, bless her heart, had always wanted a cultured musician type for a son, but she got me, and the piano lessons didn't work. That fig leaf didn't fit. My two older sisters were straight-A students, but I never saw a C that I didn't like, so a career in academia was not in the cards. But I could play football, and I could hit surprisingly hard. It was the one thing I could do, and it became my fig leaf of choice.

What I lacked in size and speed, I made up for with intensity that bordered on insanity. My high school football team was embarrassingly bad, leaving me little to feel good about except that I was a starter, and I played both on offense and defense—a very thin fig leaf, but it was better than nothing.

College football didn't seem like an option until I got a call from a Division III school in St. Paul, Minnesota, and while they weren't very good either, at least I was able to start as a college freshman—a slightly thicker fig leaf. We won only one game my freshman year, three the next year, and five the year after that. Going 5–4 was the first winning season at that school in over a decade. My senior year we went 7–2, and it was the most fun I'd ever had playing football. Division III football was a pretty small pond, but we got some attention and won some awards. I even won a couple myself to hang on my wall!

Did you know that you can hang your fig leaves on a wall?

Those experiences gave me lots of good things that I wouldn't trade for the world, but they also gave me my first conscious taste of how thin fig leaves can be. Indeed, some are so thin that people can see right through them. And they're flimsy too, because all it takes to lose one is to have somebody come along who's bigger, better, faster, and—boom—your fig leaf is gone. So you have to keep updating your fig leaf, improving it, and polishing it. But after a while, that gets exhausting.

Did you know that you can hang your fig leaves on a wall?

In her book *Transformed into Fire*, Judith Hougen provides some helpful insight into the illusory nature of this. She asserts that at the root of our false-self strategies, providing as it were the necessary fuel to keep the engine running, are two core beliefs:

First Core Belief: *I am irredeemably defective.*
Second Core Belief: *Love must be earned.*

"Whether these ideas are whispered on occasion or shouted constantly," states Hougen, "all of us have, to some degree, internalized and been wounded by such messages. To contend with these wounds, we craft a public face in order to cope, to fit in, and ultimately to find self-definition.

"We quickly learn that certain actions and emotions are applauded while others are condemned. A public self rises to handle the uncertain and even capricious world in which we find ourselves. Eventually, an overidentification with these outward behaviors comprises the conscious mind's sense of identity. If, for instance, you're good at sports, your skills might form a core of how you think about yourself. If you're smart, your intelligence becomes the prime source of your identity. 'That's who I am,' you think, 'the person who does these things or performs these roles.'"[22]

That's the problem with fig leaves. It's not that they're patently evil; it's that if you're using them as a source of identity, or as a way to be protected and clothed, they don't work. At best, they're illusory. They might look good for a while, but even the shiny and updated ones have very little substance, so they do very little good, and the maintenance is crazy.

But some people can do that for a very long time. Indeed, some people spend their entire lives adjusting, improving, and replacing their fig leaves. No wonder they're breathless.

Breaking the Cycle

What then has the power to loosen the grip of the impostor and break the cycle of adjusting and polishing our leaves? For some, it's the fatigue. They allowed their chronic breathlessness to get their attention, and they finally said, "Enough! I need some air!"

Most people don't figure it out on their own. We don't just wake up on a Tuesday and say, "Okay, *today* is the day I step out from behind my false self and fully reveal the real John or Dave."

It frequently takes a triggering event. Sometimes it's expected, even planned—retirement, empty nesting, or graduation. More often it's unexpected—an illness, death, divorce, or scandal. COVID-19 is a global triggering event that has caused scores of people to be wrenched from behind their fig leaves. In fact, the coronavirus isn't creating a "new normal" as much as it is exposing the worst effects of the "old normal." Comorbidities—preexisting medical conditions, often dangerous in their own right—seem to worsen the virus's course through victims. The question is, what comorbidities in your faith, relationships, business, or health are exposed in the context of triggering events?

The "Oracle of Omaha," Warren Buffett, speaking on his invest-ment strategy, once quipped, "It's only when the tide goes out that you learn who has been swimming naked." That certainly applies to how the receding tide of a triggering event can reveal what's truly behind the fig leaves we've all been hiding behind. It can leave us naked and ashamed.

Cringeworthy Fig Leaves

I don't know if this is comforting or depressing, but we're all swimming in the same soup. No one is above the fray, immune somehow from this "common to humankind" struggle with the false self. Every one of us is shadowed with an illusory self, a false self.

But the truth is that not everyone is able to see or is willing to acknowledge the reality of it. When someone does, it's always good to hear their story. It reminds us that it can be done, and it breaks the sense of isolation that we sometimes feel, as if we're the only ones who struggle with this. Stories about people who did it, and what it was like for them, are encouraging as a breath of fresh air. One of my favorites is the apostle Paul's story that he shares with surprising candor in Philippians 3.

As if coming clean at an Alcoholics Anonymous support group, Paul confesses his lifelong inclination to create a false-self persona to hide behind. In verse 4, he says, "If anyone had a mind (an inclination) to put confidence in the flesh (the false self), I far more." In other words, "You don't know anyone more inclined to put confidence in their ability to create good-looking fig leaves than me. I drank the Kool-Aid. I was all in. I far more than you!"

Then in verse 5, as if providing proof, he lays out his credentials (his fig leaves), saying, "See for yourself. Here they are. These are the external emblems of success that I worked my whole life to create. These are what I believed would clothe and protect me."

> I was circumcised the eighth day, of the nation of
> Israel, of the tribe of Benjamin, a Hebrew of Hebrews;
> as to the Law, a Pharisee; as to zeal, a persecutor of

the church; as to righteousness which is in the Law,
found blameless (Philippians 3:5–6 NASB).

The first and most obvious thing we notice is that none of the fig leaves on Paul's list would be on our list. Indeed, there's a cringe factor involved when Paul unabashedly declares that he was circumcised on the eighth day. Who goes around bragging about that? Or what nation you're from, or what tribe, or being a Hebrew of Hebrews—who cares?

But that's the whole point. In a different time and culture, our fig leaves might be different, but they are all paper-thin and flimsy. When seen through the lens of history, some of them are laughable. I imagine that Paul would think my football fig leaf to be ridiculous. He'd be asking, "Seriously, who goes around bragging about that?"

Paul grew up in a culture when a religious pedigree was the most prestigious fig leaf you could have. Growing up in a place called Tarsus, Paul's ambitions would never have included making the football team, but an advanced degree from the University of the Pharisees—yessiree, he'd take that fig leaf all day long.

It's a horrifying thing when you see that everything you built your life on is an illusion.

And behind those emblems of success, those figs leaves that were the ones you wanted to wear at that time, Paul felt fully clothed. He was successful and secure and in control . . . or so he believed.

Until one day on the road to Damascus in Acts 9, fully clothed in the certainty that his religious fig leaves provided, Paul received what we would call "a rude awakening." It was the bright light of reality, and in a flash he saw his fig leaves for what they were—paper-thin, flimsy veneers. It's a horrifying thing when you see that everything you built your life on is an illusion. The bright light of reality had flattened him, leaving him blind and completely undone. He didn't know up from down. He didn't know anything for sure. Not anymore. He was blind in every sense of the word.

Third-Day Stories

We're told that Paul was blind for three days: "He was three days without sight, and neither ate nor drank"(Acts 9:9 NASB).

There's a thing about "three days" all through the Scriptures. Jonah, for example, was in the belly of the whale for three days. Jesus was raised from the dead on the third day. Indeed, there are what have come to be known as "third-day stories," and they all have the same pattern and rhythm, even the same point.

> The *First Day* is a really bad day. It's the "Oh, no" day. It's the day Jonah gets swallowed by a whale and Jesus gets nailed to a cross. It's the "everything is lost" day.

> The *Second Day* is worse than the first day. The finality starts to sink in. Christ really is dead. The marriage really is over. My career really is done. My health really is failing. But the second day is also the day that God is at work in ways you could not know and did not see.

> The *Third Day* is the day that belongs to God. It's the day when God shows up and begins to breathe life.

It's the day when stubborn prophets, such as Jonah, get dropped off at seaside ports by very large fish. And harem girls, such as Esther, face down kings to save a nation. And a rabbi named Jesus is raised from the dead.

When the Scriptures say that Paul was blind for three days, it may have been three actual days, but it doesn't have to be because this is a third-day story. And what that means is that the first day, the light from heaven flashed around him and blinded him. It was an "Oh, no" day. "Help! I'm exposed! I'm naked!"

The second day was worse, because it began to sink in on Paul: "I've spent my whole life wrapped in these fig leaves." And while Paul's second day was only for a day, you and I may have experienced second days that last for weeks, or months, or years. Sometimes the second day is a very, very long day.

But in all the third-day stories, God is at work on the second day in ways you cannot see until the third day. And the third day—that's a great day! Because the lights come on, and hope is restored. We can breathe again.

The Moment of Truth

Paul's third day began with what we would call a "moment of truth." When the bright light of reality revealed something he hadn't seen before, Paul had some choices to make. They were critical choices—life-and-death choices. We have the same options at our moment of truth.

Our first option: RETREAT. This is a very popular option. You simply accept the fact that you're a fraud. Your fig leaves are proof that it's over for you, your cover is blown, so you take your place at the end of the line.

I grew up reciting in church *every* Sunday that I was a "poor, miserable sinner." While perhaps theologically accurate (original sin and all), the corrosive nature of that weekly profession of inherent unworthiness had a deep and long-lasting damaging impact on me. Living that belief makes Option 1 the natural default option. It ignores the fact that we're not simply sinners, but *deeply loved* sinners. As David Benner beautifully points out, "The sequence is important. We must never confuse the secondary fact with the primary truth."[23]

Our second option: REBUILD. This is the most popular option. You simply and quietly pick up the pieces and begin to *rebuild* your false self. You endure the initial humiliation of exposure of your fig leaf, but then work harder than ever to repair it and quickly sew it back on.

Our third option: REPENT and BELIEVE. This option brings a breath of fresh air. Press pause here for an important clarification about the word *repent*. It's a dusty old word, and for some it's repellent, stirring images of a long bony finger being waved in our face full of judgment. Or there's that crazy guy on a street corner screaming into a crappy microphone, "REPENT now or burn in HELL!"

As a preacher/teacher, I love taking misunderstood words like this and redeeming them, because *repent* is a great word and I want it back. To be sure, it can be used in a censorious way that makes people cringe, but at its root it simply means "to change your mind and turn." So repent and believe, which we identify as the third and most life-giving option, simply means to change your mind and believe that the gospel is true.

Frederick Buechner says it this way: "Repent and believe that the gospel is true, Jesus says. Turn around and believe the good news that we are loved [by God for free] is better than we ever dared hope, and that to believe in that good news . . . is of all glad things in this world the gladdest thing of all."[24]

So repent! Change your mind, and forcefully reject the lies you've believed about your value, and where it comes from, and that who you are is determined by how you look or perform. Those are lies from hell, and if you believe them, even a little, you need to repent.

And change your mind about retreating into hopelessness or replacing your fig leaves with new ones. You've had enough of that life! This really is an invitation into a new kind of life, an entirely new way of living, including what you value and how you keep score.

The transformation doesn't happen overnight. It might very well be a third-day story. But you can *change your mind* overnight. You can change your *direction* overnight. You can do that right now!

All you have to do is *turn*. And then turn again, and then again, and again. Keep on turning, and little by little, you'll notice something you didn't expect—you're breathing again. Your breathing is easy again. Like in the beginning.

> *Change your mind, and forcefully reject the lies you've believed about your value, and where it comes from, and that who you are is determined by how you look or perform.*

Time to Decide

So do you RETREAT? REBUILD? Or REPENT? You need to decide, and then act.

Henri Nouwen describes it this way: "When the night is bad, and my nerves are shattered and infinity speaks, when God Almighty shares through His Son the depth of His feelings for me, when His love flashes into my soul and when I am overtaken by Mystery—it is *kairos* [time to decide].

"Shivering in the rags of my wintry years, either I escape into skepticism and intellectualism, or with radical amazement I surrender in faith to the truth of my belovedness."[25]

Before you can breathe deeply, however, you may need to realize some of the air you're currently breathing is toxic. You might even be intentionally choosing to breathe it.

READ—REFLECT—RESPOND

Chapter Three: Bad Breath

THEME: *We all wear fig leaves*

READ the following Scriptures:

- ☐ Philippians 4:4–7
- ☐ Galatians 6:12
- ☐ Genesis 3

REFLECT on the following questions:

- ☐ Can you identify your "go to" fig leaf?
- ☐ What is your most embarrassing fig leaf?
- ☐ How closely aligned is your *form* with your *essence*?
- ☐ Can you remember the first time you found yourself hiding?
- ☐ What gives you, or has given you, the courage to remove the fig leaf?

RESPOND to the following challenge:

- ☐ Spend some time in silence and ask God where in your life you need to repent.

We can't attack those people; they are stronger than we are. We seemed like grasshoppers in our own eyes, and we looked small to them.

Numbers 13

The Sea of Galilee has an outlet. It gets to give. It gathers in its riches that it may pour them out again to fertilize the Jordan plain. But the Dead Sea with the same water makes horror. For the Dead Sea has no outlet. It gets to keep.

Harry Emerson Fosdick

CHAPTER 4

The Air You Breathe

My wife, Carol, and I were baptized in the Jordan River in fall 2018. It was a transformational experience on every level. As we stepped into the same waters that John used to baptize Jesus, a group of fifty Filipino men and women were singing songs of praise in their own language as they were being baptized next to us. Just as we were immersed in the water, they broke into "Amazing Grace" in English! We felt as if we had miraculously been transported to the green room of heaven.

About ninety-three miles downstream from that life-giving spot, the Jordan River empties into the Dead Sea, which is more picturesque than the muddy Jordan. Deep greenish-blue in color and surrounded by rolling hills, it makes for spectacular photos. But being the lowest point on earth, with its 34 percent salinity, it is, as the name states, *dead*. Nothing lives in the Dead Sea.

Why? The Jordan River is alive because water flows through it. The Dead Sea is barren because it has no outlet. Water flows in from the Jordan and never leaves except through slow evaporation.

As Harry Emerson Fosdick observed over a century ago, "The Sea of Galilee has an outlet. It gets to give. It gathers in its riches that it may pour them out again to fertilize the Jordan plain. But the Dead Sea with the same water makes horror. For the Dead Sea has no outlet. It gets to keep."[26]

The key to life is input *and* output. *Healthy* input and output.

The same is true for breathing. There's really no mystery to the rhythm of breathing: Breathe in—Breathe out—Repeat.

As we breathe in, oxygen enters the lungs and diffuses into the blood. It is taken to the heart and pumped into the cells. At the same time, the carbon dioxide waste from the breakdown of sugars in the cells of the body diffuses into the blood, then from the blood into the lungs, and is expelled as we breathe out. One gas (oxygen) is exchanged for another (carbon dioxide).

The question is, what kind of air are you breathing? Is it good and healthy air? And are you remembering to exhale? Or are you storing up waste?

While we don't think much about our breathing or what it does, it is generally true that what's inside us will kill us if it is allowed to stay. Most of us are not aware that we produce some significantly toxic wastes that need to be eliminated. There's this incredibly important thing we do, most of the time without thinking, that takes care of all that—we exhale. We simply breathe out all the toxins that would kill us if they stayed. We do it all day long, even in our sleep, breathing in and breathing out.

Are you breathing in the grace and truth of God? And are you breathing out the lies and distortions that are toxic to your soul?

But it's not just physical breath, because we're not merely physical creatures, so we need to talk about our spiritual breathing. While sometimes its natural and easy, sometimes we forget to breathe.

78

Our question is, are you breathing in the grace and truth of God? And are you breathing out the lies and distortions that are toxic to your soul?

The Air We Breathe

The diagnostic process of my IPF (Dave) was not a short one. For two years I went to doctors and specialists about my symptoms that were getting progressively worse—the shortness of breath, light-headedness, and chronic cough. Exercise induced asthma was the first diagnosis, for which I was given an inhaler to use before my workouts. It didn't help, so I quit. We checked for mold or "something" in my workout room, because the symptoms were always worse during exercise, but we found nothing wrong with the air.

It wasn't until a CT scan of my lungs revealed the fibrosis that we finally knew what we were dealing with—idiopathic pulmonary fibrosis. There were diagnostic tests all along the way, including lung capacity tests, blood tests, X-rays, and the like. But these were always accompanied by questions about the air I'd been breathing. They were the routine questions we always get asked when we go to a doctor, but this time they were pertinent to why I was there. "What kind of air have you been breathing?"

"Do you smoke? Does anyone in your family smoke? Have you smoked in the past? Have you stopped? When did you stop? Do you work, or have you ever worked, in an environment with toxins in the air?" There were questions about family history and where I grew up. "Was there asbestos in the house? Did you grow up on a landfill full of nuclear waste? Are any of your siblings mutants?" (Yes! All of them are. I'm the only one who's not, but that's another story!)

They asked me questions I would never have thought to ask, but they were all asking the same thing: *What kind of air have you been breathing, and how long have you been breathing it?*

Have you ever stopped to ask that of yourself?

Thinking About What We Don't Think About

We breathe in and out, all day long, all our lives, even when we sleep . . . until we can't. And then we are forced to think about our breathing.

Most of the time we don't think about the air we breathe, because we don't need to. We just breathe it, assuming that it's safe. But if your lungs begin to burn and you suddenly start to cough, you start paying attention. Suddenly you're thinking about the air you breathe. The air that makes you cough is obviously toxic, and you instinctively know to stop breathing that air, take evasive action, get out of the room, open a window, or put on a mask. You'd never intentionally breathe in toxic air, so when you know it's there, you find some way to avoid breathing it.

The coronavirus suddenly has everybody thinking about the air we breathe, because it could be carrying a potentially fatal disease without a person even knowing it. Masks have become the must-have fashion accessory of the day!

But what if you can't avoid it? What if there's no escape? What if the only air you have to breathe where you live is polluted? That's not a hypothetical thing, because there are places in the world where the pollution is so thick you can see it. It literally blocks out the sun. It's the only air people have to breathe.

I was in Shanghai several years ago when I was stuck in traffic for an hour in a tunnel as we traveled from one part of the city to another. The air quality was so bad that you could not only see it but taste it. It had a beautiful blue hue to it, but it burned my throat and lungs with every breath until we escaped the tunnel.

The Toxic Air We Can't Avoid

As frightening a scenario as that might be in different parts of the world, it's not the reality for most of us, because the air we breathe every day is relatively clean. We can sympathize greatly with their plight, but we can't actually relate to it. Except for the fact that we're not just talking about the realities of physical breathing in this book. Indeed, the primary point of the book is that we're not just physically alive. We have a *spiritual* life.

We are all *living souls*.

So what if the living soul that you are grew up in a home or went to a school or

Are there lies you've been breathing in, maybe for years, about who God is, and who you are, and how life works, that are colorless and odorless, that seem harmless, but they're not?

even a church where the only air you had to breathe was toxic? What if that air was so thick with pollution that it blocked out the Son? Full of lies or distortions about who God is, and who you are, and what you're worth. And while some of them were blatant (making them easier to spot and ultimately reject), others were subtle (making them harder to spot and ultimately reject). But it's where you lived, so there was no escape. It's the only air you had to breathe.

That's a scary thought. All of us grew up *somewhere*, where the air we had to breathe might not have been good for a little kid to be breathing, but it's the only air we had to breathe. And we had to breathe it for eighteen or more years.

Let's make eighteen years the magic number. Let's say when you're eighteen you go off to college, or join the military, or get married. It's a way to escape. The first thing you feel is relief, like a blast of mountain fresh air. You can finally breathe, and the breathing is easy. You can finally start living free!

But is that the way it really works? Is it actually possible to breathe toxic air for eighteen years, every day, all day, and then just walk away and start breathing easy? Perhaps it's possible to walk away with your soul intact after eighteen years of breathing toxic air . . . but not likely. That would be similar to a lifetime smoker who smokes six packs of cigarettes a day and dies of natural causes at the age of ninety-nine. Possible, but not likely.

I (John) had a client once whose business was a brewery. It actually was a sweet deal because one of the perks was free beer. They even had a tap in the lobby of their corporate headquarters. It was totally acceptable to have a pint while waiting for an appointment. Morning. Afternoon. It made no difference.

But later this business was acquired by a tobacco company. Then, in addition to drinking, smoking was not only accepted, it was expected of anyone who wanted to advance up the corporate ladder. Leadership development sessions were held in windowless rooms with three quarters of the participants smoking their way to promotions. After a year, we let them go as a client to avoid ruining our lungs. We could choose the clients with whom we worked. But many aspiring leaders in that company felt they had no choice as to the air they were breathing. They just couldn't avoid it.

The Toxic Air We Can't Smell

Add to that this possibility: Could you be breathing in toxic air and *not* know it or choose it? Like a spiritual version of carbon monoxide that's colorless and odorless, could you be breathing in things that can kill your soul and not even know it? Are there lies you've been breathing in, maybe for years, about who God is, and who you are, and how life works, that are colorless and odorless, that seem harmless, but they're not?

What about the cultural air you're breathing? Is it healthy? Are you even aware of it?

In what has become a famous college commencement address, David Foster Wallace opened with this story: "There are these two young fish swimming along, and they happen to meet an older fish swimming the other way, who nods at them and says, 'Morning, boys, how's the water?' The two young fish swim on for a bit, and then eventually one of them looks over at the other and goes, 'What the hell is water?'"[27]

Toxic air (lies about who we are) has a profound effect on who we think we are. We are often so busy, distracted, overwhelmed, or gasping for breath that we don't even recognize the high level of cultural toxicity. The air we are breathing doesn't smell, but it looks and sounds like this:

Identity: You are what you produce. How you look is
what matters most.

Wealth: You've earned it. It's yours. More is better. There's only so much in the world, so grab as much as you can for yourself.

Work: Leisure beats work. Work only as long as you have to and as hard as you must. You're accountable only to yourself.

Generosity: You're on your own. Everyone for himself. What you have is for your own enjoyment. If you don't have enough, it's your own fault.

All of these cultural lies are like carbon monoxide—silent killers of your soul. What if instead you begin to breathe in this fresh air:

Identity: You are outrageously loved by an outrageously loving God. You have infinite worth and are a citizen of heaven, free from condemnation, and the masterpiece of God.

Wealth: All things are created and owned by God (Psalm 50:10), and He abundantly provides all that we need (John 10:10). You have to make a choice between God and mammon (Luke 16:13).

Work: Work diligently with all that God provides (Proverbs 21:5) and take a patient, long-term perspective (Proverbs 31:11).

Generosity: A healthy relationship with God and others is the source of contentment, not money or possessions (Ecclesiastes 5:10). Gratitude is the healthy response (Colossians 3:16).

Are you smelling the air you're breathing?

The Toxic Air We Can't Live Without

Add one more question: Are there lies you've been breathing in for so long that you have actually come to like them? If you're a smoker, for instance, you get used to the smell in your house. You don't even notice it. You might even *like* it, because it smells like home. You're not running for your life to get away from that toxic air—no, you actually prefer it.

My cigarette smoking friends breathe in smoke that even they admit could kill them, but they still smoke. Weird, isn't it? It feels so good that they do it regardless.

My dad (John) was a three pack-a-day guy for many years and obviously addicted to the sensation of smoking. But he had to have his gallbladder removed back in the day when that was a weeklong recovery process in the hospital. Halfway through the week, he snuck out of his room to catch a smoke in the stairwell. An orderly happened upon him, snatched the cigarette out of his mouth, stubbed it out with his foot, and rebuked my dad, "Are you *crazy*, man? You're smoking while recovering from surgery? Don't you know that could kill you?"

That wasn't on my dad's mind. He just wanted his smoke. He was used to it. It is possible to enjoy toxic air, even if it kills us.

So what might be the spiritual equivalent of breathing in lies that we know could kill us, but we no longer care? Well, we know that our anger is killing us (not to mention our marriage), but we might no longer care, because it also protects us. We just keep smoking it. And we know that our need to control and always be right continually ruins relationships, but we might keep breathing in the pride and arrogance that fuels all that. We just keep "lighting up."

Who Do You Think You Are?

How does all of this bad air impact our soul?

I hadn't known Aaron very well or for very long, but from a distance he was one of those guys who seemed to have the deck stacked in his favor. He was good-looking, athletic, funny, smart, and accomplished at whatever he wanted to do. From a distance he seemed to be at ease with himself, and from a distance it seemed obvious as to why. He had it all.

But like the view you have from the highway of a family farm

How does all of this bad air impact our soul?

that looks pristine, you don't see the mud and the mess and the broken fences, and you don't smell the hog barn that tells a different story until you drive up the driveway. Aaron's actual life told a different story of insecurity, striving, and never feeling like he was enough. No one who knew him thought that about him. But he did.

It's who Aaron thought he was. And I love this guy, so I want to honor him in how I say this, but it didn't take much digging to uncover the story of a father who had communicated to him in a variety of ways, for years, that he didn't have what it takes—that he *wasn't* enough. It was the only air he had to breathe from his dad. It's where he lived. Now that's who he thought he was: "I am not enough."

But that was a lie! A toxic lie that he had been breathing into the depths of his soul for many years. The good news for Aaron is that he began to see that it was just that—a lie. Through the help of some good friends and a wife who saw more in him than he could see in himself, he began to breathe different air, and he started coming back to life. (Somebody shout "Hallelujah!")

Our question is, who do you think you are?

Grasshoppers in Our Own Sight

There's a great story in Numbers 13, where the people of God are on the shores of the Jordan River about to cross over into the Promised Land. The symbolism here is significant because this is "dream come true" stuff. It's the fulfillment of their destiny. Everything they've been thinking about and hoping for is finally here. They're crossing over into a whole new kind of life, and it's full of milk and honey.

They sent spies to check the place out, because they didn't know what they were up against. But the spies came back with good and bad news. On one hand, they said, "The land is exactly what we were promised—a land flowing with milk and honey. But the cities are fortified and very large, and the people who live there are huge, even giants. *We felt like grasshoppers in our own sight.*" In other words, "We don't have a chance! We probably shouldn't even try." So they didn't.

What's fascinating and actually quite telling about this story is that they *saw themselves* as grasshoppers. As far as we know, nobody called them grasshoppers, and if they had, they might have been offended. They had become *like* grasshoppers in *their own sight*. It's how they saw themselves. *We are insignificant. Incapable. Small.* People like that generally don't take possession of much of anything. They're grasshoppers!

But how did they get like this? You don't have to be a psychologist to know that living as slaves for four hundred years in Egypt had everything to do with it. Their fathers, and their grandfathers, and great-grandfathers had breathed the toxic air of slavery, and that has a way of getting inside. Particularly as it relates to identity. "It's who we are. It's who we've been. It's who we'll always be. It's how we see *ourselves*. We are like grasshoppers."

So how do you see yourself?

Which is to say, "We are *insignificant,* we are *incapable,* and we are *small.* We are *not enough.*"

So how do you see yourself?

Don't You Know Who I Am?

Of course, rather than having our head and heart filled with messages of how insignificant, incapable, or small we are, we can be surrounded by sycophants who fill us with a distorted view of our "totally awesomeness." This is even a more destructive toxin.

"You're not a grasshopper. You are a god or goddess! You eat grasshoppers for breakfast. Every day!"

The stories are legion of business moguls, celebrities, and athletes who have a posse of adoring followers who fill them with head trash in return for scraps that fall off the table of their exalted status. The overused phrase "It's lonely at the top" not only refers to a physical isolation, it also refers to a tendency for truth to never reach the corporate top floor or fly on the private jet.

Andy Crouch says, "Among the many dark gifts of power is distance—distance from accountability, distance from consequences, distance from the pain we cause others, distance from self-knowledge, distance from friendship, distance from the truth. The palace rooftop, the back entrance, the executive bathroom, the private jet—the accommodations that hide us from others' sight."[28]

The flip side of "Who do you think you are?" is "Don't you know who I am?" Google that phrase and you'll find highly publicized failures. That classic question almost always immediately precedes an epic fall from some exalted status. A perp walks in cuffs, bankruptcy, or worse yet, death.

My personal favorite is of a pro athlete who was ripping around Atlanta in a Lamborghini killing time before dinner. When he was pulled over for failing to signal while switching lanes, he told the officer, "Take the vehicle. I have ten more!" The officer would have none of it and wouldn't let the athlete just leave the car, resulting in the obligatory, "Don't you know who I am?" The cop didn't care.

It's easy to poke fun at these glaring failures, but honestly, haven't you at least had the same thought at some point in your life? We may never drive a Lamborghini, but aren't we all most vulnerable to suck in this toxic air right after a big and perhaps unexpected success?

A good friend cautioned me after I had given a speech to the largest gathering in my career, "Guard your heart today. Don't let pride in. Give God the glory for the gap between how good you *really* are at this and how great it went."

That was great advice, and much-needed. The day immediately after a significant high is often the most dangerous day. We are easily fooled into believing it is all about us. We can become "legends in our own minds" and at least think, if not utter, the killer phrase, "Don't you know who I am?"

The Only Way Out Is Through

What's the treatment for toxic air, whether it is seen or unseen, forced upon us or chosen, or even liked? How do we begin to breathe in the fresh air of truth?

James, in the epistle that bears his name, says that "wisdom from above is first of all pure [that is to say true], then it is peaceable." That means the only way to peace is *through* the truth.

So what is the truth about the toxic air you've been breathing? Do you know? Have you thought about the toxic air you breathe, and how long you've been breathing it?

So what is the truth about the toxic air you've been breathing? Do you know? Have you thought about the toxic air you breathe, and how long you've been breathing it?

This may be different, and we don't want to lose you here, but we're closing this chapter with an assignment for you to do. We think that the best way for you to do it might be with some trusted friends, perhaps someone you can talk with in confidence, maybe even your small group, but it's work that we believe will be worth doing.

We're keeping this simple. Three things. Remember, breathing is as simple as Breathe in—Breathe out—Repeat.

1. *Breathe In*—the truth about who God is, and who you are, and how life works.

   Breathe in Reality
   • That God is light and in Him there is no darkness at all.

- That God is good and actually cares about you.
- That God's kingdom matters more than yours. (It's not all about you—*really*!)
- That life is hard, you're not in control, and you're going to die.
- That your name has been written in the Book of Life, so you are eternally significant.

Breathe in Identity

- That you are an unceasing, spiritual being with an eternal destiny in God's great universe.
- That you are not a human being having a spiritual experience. You are a spiritual being having a brief human experience.
- That you are outrageously loved by an outrageously loving God.

2. *Breathe Out*—the toxic lies you've been holding inside.

Can you name the toxic air you had to breathe as a kid?

- It was the only air you had to breathe.
- There was no escape. It's where you lived.

Can you name the toxic air that was colorless and odorless?

- It's the air we breathe from the culture and often from the church.
- It doesn't make us cough because it's not obviously repugnant.

Can you name the toxic air that you've embraced as if it were your friend?

- You know it may kill you or your relationships, but you don't care anymore.
- This one requires enormous courage and desire you may not yet have. We hope you can find it.

3. *Repeat*

Let's start with an inhaler. Remember the inhaler that the doctor prescribed for Dave? You know, the one that didn't work? This one might just work for you. Start thinking about the things you might need to be inhaling—intentionally inhaling—every day, week, month, and year.

- Where are the places you need to go (such as a church that reveals the light to you)?
- What are the books you need to read (that bring you deeper hope and infuse you with life)?
- What are the relationships that you might need to jettison (because they're not on the same journey)?
- Which relationships need to be developed (because they are life-giving, and no one can do it alone)?
- All these things are your inhaler.

So figure that out! Start breathing the kind of air that you need to heal, grow, and become all you were created to be. Breathe in—Breathe out—Repeat. And as you do, you begin the process of recovering your breath.

READ—REFLECT—RESPOND

Chapter Four: The Air We Breathe

THEME: *The toxic air we breathe*

READ the following Scriptures:

- ☐ Philippians 4:8–9
- ☐ Luke 6:43–45
- ☐ Proverbs 4:23
- ☐ Ephesians 4:14–15

REFLECT on the following questions:

- ☐ What kind of air did you breathe in the home you grew up in?
- ☐ What is the quality of the air that you breathe every day?
- ☐ Are you able to identify the source of any toxic air you breathe?
- ☐ What kind of long-term effects has the air you've been breathing had on your soul?
- ☐ Have you grown comfortable with, or even come to prefer, air that you know to be toxic?

RESPOND to the following challenge:

To purify the air we breathe requires intentionality:
- ☐ Practice the breathing exercise we closed this chapter with: Breathe in—Breathe out—Repeat.

☐ To purify the air we breathe requires the Spirit.

☐ Make these prayers your prayers each day:

"That the eyes of your heart may be enlightened, so that you will know what is the hope of His calling, what are the riches of the glory of His inheritance in the saints, and what is the surpassing greatness of His power to those who believe" (Ephesians 1:18–19 NASB).

"For this reason I bow my knee before the Father, from whom every family in heaven and on earth derives its name, that He would grant you, according to the riches of His glory, to be strengthened with power through His Spirit in the inner man, so that Christ may dwell in your hearts through faith; and that you, being rooted and grounded in love, may be able to comprehend with all the saints what is the breadth and length and height and depth, and to know the love of Christ which surpasses knowledge, that you may be filled up to all the fullness of God" (Ephesians 3:14–19 NASB).

My soul in silence waits for God alone.

Psalm 62

*If we do not allow for a rhythm of rest in our overly
busy lives, illness becomes our Sabbath—our pneumonia,
our cancer, our heart attack, our accidents
create Sabbath for us.*

Wayne Muller

Recovering Your Breath

We called it a "sabbatical," primarily because we didn't know what else to call it. That was better than alternatives such as a "leave of absence" or an "extended vacation." A sabbatical sounded professional at least.

You may recall from Chapter Two, the discernment of the elders had been that I wasn't just out of gas, I was out of oil. In some sense, it was an intervention when they said, "The sabbatical begins today, effective immediately." Initially, I was relieved and certainly grateful for their care, but I was also overwhelmed. Taking a sabbatical had never been on my radar as a viable option, so when I suddenly found myself *on one*, it didn't feel right. Similar to waking up from a weird dream, I was disoriented and confused, wondering, *What do I do now?*

"Go home" was the only instruction they gave me. But almost immediately the voices in my head started to chatter with questions and accusations, such as, "Who gets to go home and take three months off because they're tired? Take a nap if you're tired. You can rest when you're dead. Just take a vacation. How will you explain this to your friends and family? None of them ever took a sabbatical. They will never understand."

My pastor dad, who'd always been my biggest fan, feared I would lose the church. He simply had no category into which a sabbatical might fit, especially one that seemed out of the blue because of fatigue, or burnout, or whatever we were calling it. You don't go home. That's not the way life works.

Life works when you work! "No pain, no gain" had always been the mantra. Push harder. Do more. Keep going. Never ever stop! But now, I had to stop. I was forced to stop—not just by the board, but by myself. I couldn't breathe. If I didn't figure out a way to recover my breath, I might be stopping for good.

It's ironic, because it was that fear-filled chatter that helped clarify what I needed to do. My biggest concern was no longer losing my job or the church, or even the approval of my family and friends. It was that if I kept my job and continued to do it the way I'd been doing it, I might lose my health, or my heart, or my marriage, or even something in my soul.

So How Is It with Your Soul?

"How is it with your soul?" That's not a question that comes up in casual conversation, thank goodness! But it's a great question to ask, at least of yourself.

The *soul* comes up frequently in the Scriptures, and almost a third of the time in the Psalms. "My soul waits in silence for God only" (Psalm 62:1 NASB). "I have composed and quieted my soul; like a weaned child rests against his mother, my soul is like a weaned child within me" (Psalm 131:2 NASB).

I'm struck by the fact that the psalmists could talk about their soul. They were aware of its stirrings and could name the things it felt.

They said, "My soul sings, rejoices, is troubled, is thirsty, is still, is in anguish, is refreshed, is grieved, is downcast, is awakened, is resting, is yearning, is praising, and is weary." It's as if they had some say in the condition of their soul. "And so my soul in silence waits."

John Ortberg describes the soul this way: "Your soul is what integrates your will (your intentions), your mind (your thoughts and feelings, your values and conscience), and your body (your face, body language, and actions) into a single life."[29]

The etymology of the word *integrates* is from *integer*, which means "to be whole, complete in itself." It's where we also get the word *integrity*. We are acting with integrity—as a whole person—when our soul is healthy and well-ordered. When we are out of breath, our whole being begins to *disin*tegrate. We come apart. We break down. If our soul is unhealthy, we cannot help or effectively lead anybody else.

> *In that place at the center of you, where you live with yourself, how is it with you there?*

So how is it with your soul? In that place at the center of you, where you live with yourself, how is it with you there?

Hoo-ha for the Soul

In his book *A Hidden Wholeness*, Parker Palmer likens the human soul to that of a wild animal. He observes that "like a wild animal, the soul is tough, resilient, resourceful, savvy, and self-sufficient; it knows how to survive in hard places. . . . Yet despite its toughness, the soul is shy. Just like a wild animal, it seeks safety in the dense underbrush, especially when people are around. If you want to see a wild animal, we know that the last thing we should do is go crashing through the woods, yelling for it to come out. But if we walk quietly into the woods, sit patiently at the base of a tree, breathe with the earth, and fade into our surroundings, the wild creature we seek might put in an appearance."[30]

There was a time, and not so long ago, when sentiments such as this sounded like hoo-ha to me. The thought of sitting at the base of a tree and "breathing with the earth," seriously? The perspective I held for years with regard to the spiritual practices of silence and solitude, as well as the spiritually rooted rhythms of work and rest, was that they were great for a certain *type* of person. That meant someone who had nothing to do and plenty of time on their hands, especially old people and retired people. It required the contemplative types who actually *like* sitting still, being quiet and alone, perhaps for days.

But in the reality of the rough-and-tumble world of business, commerce, work, and simply life, you actually have to *do* things, *accomplish* and *produce* things. For me, sitting quietly for hours didn't seem helpful and certainly not necessary. In my universe, if you hope to get done what needs to get done when it needs to get done, you better get going. Now!

But as it turns out, I discovered that just the opposite is true.

Rhythms of Stress and Recovery

Jim Loehr and Tony Schwartz work with world-class athletes and high-level executives at Fortune 500 companies. They have observed that if high-performing individuals don't learn rhythms of work and rest, including rhythms of silence and solitude, they won't be high performing for long. Part of the problem, they say, is what high-performing people often believe: no pain, no gain, pedal to metal, do more, push harder, stay longer, go farther, and whatever you do, never-ever stop.

But they contend, we've got a problem because now we live in digital time. "Our rhythms are rushed, rapid fire, and relentless, our days are carved up into bits and bytes. We celebrate breadth rather than depth, quick reaction more than considered reflection. We skim across the surface, alighting for brief moments at dozens of destinations but barely remaining for long at any one. . . . We're wired up but we're melting down. . . . We survive on too little sleep, wolf down fast food on the run, fuel up with coffee and cool down with alcohol and sleeping pills. . . . We take pride in our ability to multitask, and wear our willingness to put in long hours as a badge of honor. The term *24/7* describes a world in which work never ends. We use words like obsessed, crazed, and overwhelmed not to describe insanity, but instead to characterize our everyday lives."[31]

Jared Sandberg observed in *The Wall Street Journal*, "What now passes for multitasking was once called not paying attention."[32] There's even a whole dialect to describe this insanity: deskfast, cup-holder cuisine, hurry sickness, presenteeism. In business, this excessive busyness is corrosive to reflection, which, in turn, inhibits creativity, the wellspring of breakthrough ideas and sustainable leadership. As Gary Haugen, CEO of International Justice Mission, observed, "As a leader, there is no way I can offer far-sighted steadiness in a state of breathless hurry."[33]

This is especially a problem for people of faith. Richard Foster observes, "We pant through an endless series of appointments and duties. This problem is especially acute for those who sincerely want to do what is right. With frantic fidelity we respond to *all* calls to service, distressingly unable to distinguish the voice of Christ from that of human manipulators. We feel bowed low with the burden of integrity."[34]

If you actually live that way, which was Loehr and Schwartz's primary point, you may be applauded by some for what looks like a heroic effort, but you won't be in it for long, and you certainly won't be fully engaged. When they begin their work with professional athletes, all looking to improve their performance, they don't work on their mechanics, such as their swing or their shot, they work on their rhythms of work and rest. They do intense training designed to increase their strength and capacity, followed by subsequent and intentional periods of rest for the purpose of recovery and renewal.

The Human Performance Institute confirmed that it's not stress that causes problems for leaders, it's their lack of recovery. Too much stress (without recovery) leads to health issues and burnout. However, too much recovery (with no periods of stress) will fail to expand your capacity for growth. The key is the right blend of performance and recovery for every individual.

You can keep believing, as I did, that you can ignore these "built into us by God" rhythms of work and rest, and that you'll somehow be the exception to the rule. But you do so at your peril.

As you can imagine, it is the rhythm of intentional and almost regimented rest that is the most difficult thing to accept and implement. If the only speed you know is full tilt, and if doing it that way has been working for you, you might be hesitant to buy in. That is, until you do what I did and just hit the wall. It's not very pleasant, but you can do it.

You can just keep doing what you're doing. You can keep

believing, as I did, that you can ignore these "built into us by God" rhythms of work and rest, and that you'll somehow be the exception to the rule. But you do so at your peril. As Wayne Muller warns, "If we do not allow for a rhythm of rest in our overly busy lives, illness becomes our Sabbath—our pneumonia, our cancer, our heart attack, our accidents create Sabbath for us."[35]

Doing It the Hard Way

Experience may be the best teacher, and the experiences that teach us the most are difficult ones. Richard Rohr nails it when he suggests that after the age of thirty, we learn nothing from our successes, only our failures. Success is important in the first half of life as you're building a healthy sense of self, which Rohr calls "building your tower."[36] But continued success as the golden boy who's everybody's hero and always does it right simply serves to cement certainties of which you should not be certain. And while certainty feels good, cemented certainty makes transformation impossible and wisdom will never be discovered.

Hitting the wall the way I did was not a pleasant experience, partly because I was no longer certain. It wasn't a faith crisis; it wasn't God or my faith that was being decentered. It was the certainty I had that if I just kept pushing and working and standing and pushing some more, I'd eventually prevail. It wasn't about winning, because I wasn't competing or fighting with anyone. It was about prevailing, standing, and staying. I was far less certain that I could simply *will myself* to keep going, and I was suddenly very interested in, and ready to take seriously, *anything* that might help me recover my breath.

My breathlessness had served as a kind of intervention on both

103

the arrogance and ignorance that had led me to believe I was someone above the fray. That the sacred rhythms and spiritual practices that nourish and help sustain, not only the body but the soul, are fine for some but not for me. All of that got *intervened* on when I came up gasping for breath.

My good friend Jeff VanVonderen does interventions for a living, which might sound weird. But weird or not, for several years he was one of the key players in an A&E television series called *Intervention*. Jeff was a master at calmly and methodically coaching the family or friends of an addict on how to do an intervention. The intervention itself, particularly for the person being intervened on, is not a pleasant experience. It's a bit of an ambush really, when a small group of people care enough about the addict to intervene on their behalf. Leading with love, they unwaveringly shine the bright light of truth on patterns of behavior and dysfunction that have long been denied and ignored or simply tolerated, but no longer. Now the addict's only option is treatment. Though some resist and ultimately refuse the intervention, most relent and receive it as the gift it's intended to be— to save their life. And when they do, Jeff is ready. Often the next day they're on a plane headed for a treatment center where they'll get the help they need, and now they're in *recovery*.

Hitting the wall and coming up breathless was that kind of intervention for me. When the elders said, "Stop and go home," it intervened on a lifelong pattern of never stopping, especially when things are tough. Like an alcoholic who hasn't hit bottom, I could've minimized or even denied I had a problem. I could have taken a couple days to catch my breath and then got back at it. Instead, I did what they told me: "Shut it down—now." And when I did, I began to recover my breath. I was in *recovery*.

True recovery requires three steps: Admit there's a problem ("I am overwhelmed"). Accept that there's help ("I can't do this alone"). Take the action required to move forward (In my case, invite God's Spirit in through my sabbatical).

Being in Recovery

Recovery, whether it happens at a treatment center or simply in the course of life, is not a walk in the park. You may not be going to work every day when you're in recovery, but you're working every day. On my sabbatical, I did not have one day of peaceful rest or easy breathing. I didn't know how to do either.

To recover my breath, and not just catch it, would require some work. The analogy may seem extreme, but like an alcoholic who's in for treatment, the fact that you've stopped drinking (at least while you're there) doesn't mean you've recovered. Recovery is when you start digging in the dirt of *why* you're drinking, and why you can't *stop* drinking. What's behind all of that, and what's driving all that?

You can modify your schedule and take an extra day off if it helps you catch your breath, but you won't *recover* your breath until you start digging in the dirt of *why* you keep running even when you're out of breath. For me it meant going to a counselor who would tell me the truth, and who would with grace help me identify ways of thinking and believing

You can modify your schedule and take an extra day off if it helps you catch your breath, but you won't recover your breath until you start digging in the dirt of why you keep running even when you're out of breath.

and behaving that were destructive—not just to me, but to people I loved. When you let someone start digging in your dirt like that, it'll take your breath away. But if you allow it, and if you stay in it, you'll actually begin to recover your breath. Transformation begins.

Liminal Space

In his book, *Adam's Return,* Richard Rohr says that all transformation takes place in what he refers to as liminal space,[37] which is precisely what we've been describing here. The word *liminal* comes from the Latin root *limen,* which means "threshold." When you cross a threshold, you're *crossing over* as you move from one room into the next. But the threshold itself is that place *between.* It's when you've left one room (one reality, one way of living or being that is familiar), but you haven't fully come into the new way. You're in liminal space.

That is an uncomfortable and unsettling place where nothing feels certain, but it is also a sacred space—a place of transformation. Biblically, it's seen as the wilderness or the desert. It's the belly of the whale. It's the dark night of the soul. It's the place that none of us willingly go.

Rohr says that it is into that liminal and uncertain place where the biblical God always seems to be leading His people, purposefully to keep them there long enough to learn something essential and genuinely new. And there's the rub, because we don't wait very well.

We give answers too readily, take away pain too easily, and stimulate too quickly. We are, says Rohr, at a symbolic disadvantage as a wealthy culture. The rich can satisfy their loneliness and longing in false ways, with quick fixes and easy answers that allow us to avoid the necessary learning. In terms of soul care, it's why the poor in some cultures have a head start, because they can't always find instant relief. There is no pill to take, no easy way out, no vacation to go on, no expensive toy or entertainment, and so they have to stay there in the belly of the whale. The only way out is through.

The Place of Waiting

"Sooner or later," Rohr says, "life is going to lead us (as it did Jesus) into the belly of the beast, into a place we can't fix, control, explain, or understand. That's where transformation most easily happens—because only there are we in the hands of God—and not self-managing."[38]

Whether we like it or not, understand it or not, all of us will log some time in the liminal space of the desert.

- David was anointed as king, and it should have been a straight shot to the throne, but he spent ten years running from Saul and hiding in caves in the desert (1 Samuel 16).
- The people of Israel had been liberated from Egypt, and the Promised Land was just a two-weeks' journey away, but God led them around by way of the desert for forty years (Numbers 1).
- Joseph was promised by God in a dream that he would be a ruler, and the first thing that happened in its fulfillment was to be sold by his brothers as a slave (Genesis 37).
- Jesus, having just begun His ministry, was first led by the Spirit into the wilderness for forty days (Luke 4).

We find those stories inspirational because we know how they turned out. It's great that Jonah was deposited by a smelly fish on a beach with a renewed sense of mission. Yes, David ultimately became the greatest king in Israel's history. The people of God finally arrived in the Promised Land, even though they did it on the roundabout way of the wilderness. You're glad that I am on the other side of my sabbatical with my character formed. All of it came through liminal space, and all of them are places of transformation.

I (John) have a friend named Mike who recounts his first kindergarten parent-teacher conference for his son Alex. The teacher said, "I've been doing this so long that there's nothing these kids do that can surprise me. But your Alex did! When asked, 'What do you want to be when you grow up?' Alex stood right up by his desk and proudly announced, 'I want to be an alcoholic just like my dad!' He made it sound really positive." Because, in fact, it was. Mike had been fifteen years sober at that point. Alex knew how the story turned out, at least up to that point. Sobriety was his father's answer to drunkenness.

We love these stories because we know the answers to the questions that were being asked of all the main characters. We like answers more than questions. The problem, says Henri Nouwen, is that "answers before questions do damage to the soul."[39] Transformation doesn't happen in the context of answers.

> *Transformation doesn't happen in the context of answers.*

We like standing on solid ground more than hanging out in midair. Standing in the light is so much better than being hurled into a deep abyss. We crave certainty rather than ambiguity. Unfortunately, as Brian Zahnd points out, "Certitude is a poor substitute for authentic faith. But certitude is popular; it's popular because it's easy. If all you want is cheap certitude, just land on some opinion one way or the other, tell yourself you're certain, and that's that. No wrestling with doubt, no dark night of the soul, no costly agonizing over the matter, no testing yourself with hard questions. Just accept a secondhand assumption or a majority opinion or a popular sentiment as the final word and settle into certainty. You don't have to think about it ever again. Ignorance is bliss, but so is certitude—they're first cousins. Yet none of this is to be confused with faith."[40]

Here's the challenge: We seldom plan a trip into liminal spaces. We stumble into it. We are pushed into it with a directive such as, "Dave, go home."

Or we are hurled into it. "You have IPF!"

Or God brings us into it.

However we get there, certainty goes out the window. And we have to stay in that uncomfortable place of questions and ambiguity until we have learned something essential. We likely have to go back to that space not once, but many times in our life. We are stubborn and forgetful creatures. Or we might have missed something hidden in plain sight.

It All Began in the Beginning

It's a bit embarrassing as a ministry guy like myself, who talks a lot about the Scriptures, that I had missed something so obviously central to the story of God. There it stands in full view, in the very beginning, when God had completed His work on the seventh day. It says that He *rested* (Genesis 2:2). And it says He blessed that day of rest, that *seventh day*, and He sanctified it (v. 3). As if to say, the seventh day is an important day and part of an important rhythm.

It shows up again in Exodus 20. Having just been delivered from slavery, the people of God had entered into a new way of living. No longer were they slaves, driven by taskmasters who only cared about what they could produce. God brings them back to this rhythm of work and rest, saying in effect, "I want you to take a day and treat it as a sacred day, a protected day—the seventh day." "Remember the Sabbath day to keep it holy," which means to set it apart (Exodus 20:8). He was saying, "I want you to *use* that day to rest yourself physically, to realign yourself spiritually, to remember some things gratefully, so that you can live your lives productively, even abundantly."

I love that story! God is trying to help His people *recover their breath*! It's just a baby step, but it's a step. Take a day. Just one day! Protect that day. Don't work that day. Play with your kids that day. Work in the garden that day. Make love that day! Get renewed that day. Recover your breath that day. Start with one day!

God didn't just put "Remember the Sabbath" into Moses' suggestion box. Remembering the Sabbath is commanded by God. Is there a more disobeyed or disregarded directive in the Western world today? It wasn't meant to be negotiable. It's not a "nice to do" if you can work it out in your schedule. But the command was not a restriction designed to confine, which it becomes for some, but a freedom designed for their flourishment, reminding them that they're no longer slaves to a taskmaster who cares only about what they produce.

Growing up, the equivalent of Sabbath was Sunday, the day of rest. But it was a day filled with restrictions and all the things you couldn't do, because God didn't like it when people had fun on His day. It was not only a boring day for me, but the day I got in more trouble than any other day, because I'd break yet another Sabbath Day rule.

Imagine my surprise when I learned that the Sabbath was designed to be a day of delight, filled with things that replenish the soul, give you joy, and turn your heart toward

Imagine my surprise when I learned that the Sabbath was designed to be a day of delight, filled with things that replenish the soul, give you joy, and turn your heart toward gratitude and God.

gratitude and God. It was the day to eat the best meats and drink the best wines and to be with people you loved. It's to remind you that you're no longer a slave!

So are you a slave to anything? Work? Relationships? Exercise? Religion? Sports? Sabbath would be a good day to think about that.

When Carol and I (John) were in Israel, one of the aha moments occurred when we observed two Sabbaths. In Jerusalem, the Sabbath (Shabbat) is still for the most part strictly observed. Public transportation is unavailable. If people travel, they usually walk. All the shops in Old Jerusalem are shuttered. The city is quiet. Tour buses, ubiquitous the rest of the week, are almost nonexistent.

The friends we traveled with were all equally impressed and convicted of the importance of rediscovering and practicing this vital rhythm. We decided to commit to observing the Sabbath together one day a month. But as soon as we all got out our electronic calendars and began trying to align on a day that worked for all of us, we were looking eight months into the future. We were totally busted!

The BGO (blinding glimpse of the obvious) was that we were all slaves to our busyness, whether it was family, work, leisure, travel, or whatever. None of our taskmasters were inherently bad. But we were enslaved, nonetheless. We could not commit to even one day a month, let alone one day a week, to formally recover.

Living on the Outer Edges

Pacem in Terris is a retreat center in Minnesota where you can go for silence and solitude. It's a beautiful place set deep in the woods, and you're entirely alone. You stay in a one-room hermitage cabin, with no electricity, no water, no toilet, and no shower. There is one bed, one chair, and one window to look out. No other options.

Anticipating that reality as I (Dave) drove there made me nervous, thinking I would go crazy during my stay, but I didn't. Indeed, I learned some important things. One was that I *could* do it. Another was that I discovered I had attachments to things I didn't realize I had. One was eating junk food late at night. How could I live without that? But I did, and that was an important thing to know. Even the rhythm of light and dark affected me. With no electricity in the room, when it got dark outside at 7 p.m., it was dark inside too. You'll never believe what I did. I went to bed. Did you know that people used to go to bed when it got dark? Crazy!

Instead of being driven nuts over the lack of options, I found it settled me down. I didn't have to wonder about anything, and there was nowhere else to go, so I settled in. For the ADHD person that I am, that was a big deal.

On my third day there, I got a picture in my mind that depicted how I'd been living. If you have a pen and paper, draw a circle, then put a dot in the center of the circle. That dot represents the core of who I am. It's where I live with myself. Now, on the top of the outside of the circle draw a stick figure. That stick figure is me, living on the circumference of my life—on the "outer edges."

Understand that the circumference of our life is not a bad or evil place. The circumference of our lives is where we live our lives. It's where we work and play, go to school and interact with the world. It's where we spend most of our time, and most of us have learned to function there with some level of competence.

What dawned on me as I reflected on this goofy little drawing was that overall I do pretty well on the circumference. I hold my own. I have competencies. I'm particularly good in stormy situations, when trouble starts brewing and the wind starts blowing, because I know what to do. I close my eyes, plant my feet, and I stay! I can stay in that place for a very long time.

But if I stay out on the circumference of my life too long, I lose touch with that little dot at the center of the circle, which is the core of who I am and who I want to be. And when I am no longer living from that place of centeredness, I begin to lose my breath. It's interesting to me that it's rarely been life's big storms that knock me over. I seem to handle the big things well, but sometimes as I'm handling those big things, it's something *little* that comes along to knock me over.

Pacem in Terris helped me *catch* my breath. But it also helped me realize that to fully *recover* my breath, and more importantly, to keep breathing deeply, I needed to practice a regular Sabbath rhythm and even a periodic sabbatical. Not just for *emergency use*, but to be part of a healthy rhythm that regularly (even daily) helps me recover my breath—by returning (even daily) to my center.

How do we do that?

How's Your Breathing?

Patrik Edblad says, "Did you know that your regular breathing pattern very likely is screwing up your body and its functions in a bunch of different ways? Without knowing it, you might be messing up your sleep, mood, digestion, heart, nervous system, muscles, brain, and even the development of your teeth and face structure. On the flip side are all the benefits to be had from learning how to breathe correctly. These include more energy, better health, decreased anxiety, less fear, better relationships, and just a happier life in general."[41]

Breathing matters! But it's not just *that* you breathe (breathing = alive; no breath = dead). It's *how* you breathe. The way we inhale and exhale is as important as genetics, diet, and exercise.

How's your breathing? When we are gasping for breath, we are invariably breathing through our mouth. The air is unfiltered, raw, dry, and contains viruses and bacteria. It saps the body of moisture, irritates the lungs, and increases the risk of respiratory infection. The healthiest breath is through your nostrils. Your nose is like "a little factory that refines and prepares the air coming in to be used by the body as efficiently as possible."[42]

Those nostrils of yours are the very same ones that God did and still does breathe in His Spirit. In the next chapter, we will unpack some healthy spiritual practices that not only allow you to recover your breath, but to regularly and systematically breathe in God's Spirit.

So how's your breathing?

Are you gasping for breath or breathing nice and easy, steady, from all the way down in your diaphragm—from your center—deeply inhaling God's Spirit?

When we are gasping for breath, we are the woman or man

climbing to the top of a mountain, hands on knees, trying desperately to refill their lungs. We eventually catch our breath, but as soon as we resume the climb, with the same lack of physical (or spiritual) fitness, we soon find ourselves right back to sucking air. Gasping for breath.

How do we move beyond just catching our breath, through recovery, to learning how to regularly breathe in life-giving, deep breaths?

We come back from a three-day weekend, or a time of silence at a retreat center, or a sabbatical, and within days or weeks we are gasping for breath again. All of which means we didn't actually recover our breath, we just caught it.

How do we move beyond just catching our breath, through recovery, to learning how to regularly breathe in life-giving, deep breaths? We need to relearn how to breathe properly, rhythmically, from deep within our soul. We need to invite God's Spirit into our overwhelmed life.

READ—REFLECT—RESPOND

Chapter Five: Recovering Your Breath

THEME: *Beginning to recover your breath*

READ the following Scriptures:

- ☐ Psalm 62:1–2, 5
- ☐ Psalm 131

REFLECT on the following questions:

- ☐ What things/situations most consistently leave you gasping for breath?
- ☐ Can you name some of the quick fixes that haven't work for you?
- ☐ Does the "going to treatment" metaphor work for you? Why? Why not?
- ☐ What would "going to treatment" look like for you? What would it take?
- ☐ How well do you live on the circumference of your life? How do you get back to the center?
- ☐ Describe a time when you were in liminal space. What was the outcome? What did you learn?

RESPOND to the following challenge:

☐ In keeping with the wise counsel of Loehr and Schwartz, pay attention this next week to how much time you spend "stressed—working and striving," and how much time you devote to "recovery."

☐ Remember, "Too much stress (without recovery) leads to health issues and burnout. However, too much recovery (with no periods of stress) will fail to expand your capacity for growth. The key is the right blend of performance and recovery for every individual." Are you striking the right balance for yourself?

☐ If you're dangerously tired, tell someone you trust and take action to begin recovering your breath.

Lord, teach us to pray.

Luke 11

*Step out of the traffic. Take a long, loving look
at me, your High God.*

Psalm 46

*It is only the quiet soul that can receive the words,
the tone, and the timber of another person's voice,
maybe even the voice of God.*

Cornelius Plantinga

CHAPTER 6

Learning to Breathe Deeply

It all began in the beginning with the breath—it was the breath of God, the breath of life. When God breathed into the nostrils of the dust that He had formed into man, man became a living soul. More than the animated tissues of a living body, man became a living soul. Dallas Willard states that more than a physical being, we were created as "unceasing spiritual beings with an eternal destiny in God's great universe."[43]

In the beginning it was good. It was very good. Having been filled with the breath of God, made in the likeness of God, fully alive to God, the crown of His creation was walking with God in the cool of the day, and the breathing was easy. But then the story took a tragic turn, and they forgot to breathe. What had once been so natural and easy became labored and forced, marked by starts and stops and gasping for breath. We've been gasping for breath ever since.[44]

And the breath we are longing for is not just an oxygen to carbon dioxide exchange, but Spirit—God's Spirit.

But What If . . .

What if there's a way to breathe deeply again? To breathe deeply of the presence of God, and the goodness of God, and the fullness of God—and to walk with God in the cool of the day when the breathing is easy.

What if the reason God sent His Son Jesus was to show us how to do it? What if His mission was to show ordinary human beings how they could experience the presence of God and intimacy with God, breathing deeply of the goodness of God by continually being connected to the breath of God?

What if that's how Jesus lived every moment of every day? What if His continual connection to the breath of God, and His breathing deeply of the goodness of God, is how He ministered to the multitudes, fed the five thousand, healed the sick, exposed false religion, turned over the tables of the money changers, and proclaimed with confidence that the kingdom of heaven is within our reach?

What if He immersed Himself in certain practices, such as silence and solitude, fasting and prayer, and even celebration, to keep Himself continually connected to the source of His breath? What if that's how He learned to breathe deeply? What if that's how He even went to the cross—breathing deeply of the goodness of God all the way home?

What if we can learn to do the same?

Practices Takes Practice

Dallas Willard, in *The Spirit of the Disciplines*, observes, "It is part of the misguided and whimsical condition of humankind that we so devoutly believe in the power of effort-at-the-moment-of-action alone to accomplish what we want and completely ignore the need for character change in our lives as a whole. The general human failing is to want what is right and important, but at the same time not commit to the kind of life that will produce the action we know to be right and the condition we want to enjoy. . . . We intend what is right, but we avoid the life that would make it reality."[45]

Jesus learned to breathe deeply, not with effort-at-the-moment-of-action alone, but by arranging His life around practices that enabled Him to do it when He most needed to be able to do it.

Jesus learned to breathe deeply, not with effort-at-the-moment-of-action alone, but by arranging His life around practices that enabled Him to do it when He most needed to be able to do it. As it turns out, He was able to breathe deeply all the way to the cross.

David Brenner asserts that "Jesus' spiritual disciplines were meaningful only in light of the primacy of His relationship with the Father. They were vehicles of communion, venues of intimacy."[46] The same is true for us.

We have identified five of those practices to start with, and we'll unpack them as best we can. But the key will be to practice. The purpose is to withdraw even for a short time from the clamor of the world and seek a sacred intimacy with the Almighty—to truly *BE* with God, just as Jesus modeled being with His Father. These are not primarily things to achieve as they are ways to prepare us to be deeply connected with the Father.

Silence

In one of the most powerful scenes in the movie *A Beautiful Day in the Neighborhood*, Mister Rogers (Tom Hanks) asks an investigative journalist (Matthew Rhys) to take a minute and think about all the people who loved him into being. Just one minute of silence.

The entire restaurant in which they are sitting falls silent, and the movie screen becomes completely still. No background noise. No musical score. Complete silence. Halfway through, Tom Hanks slowly shifts his gaze from the journalist to the viewers in the theater. To me. That's when I became completely aware of the uniqueness of that moment. Complete silence. In a movie theater. For an entire sixty seconds!

It's not just a poignant scene in that movie. Mister Rogers practiced that moment of silence in real life, including when he accepted the Lifetime Achievement Award from the National Academy of Television Arts and Sciences. He humbly asked the assembled soap opera stars and talk show hosts to pause for ten seconds of silence to remember all the people who helped them become who they are—"those who cared about you and wanted what was best for you in life." He then glanced at his watch and said gently, "I'll watch the time."

In those ten seconds, uncomfortable snickering turned to quiet tears as people throughout the hall began to silently remember impactful people who had loved and mentored them. In just ten seconds.

Turn Down the Volume

We live in a very noisy world, with a dissonance of voices that push us, and pull us, and promise us anything we want. But in the course of our everyday lives, and the speed with which we live them, and the noise that never wanes, we get easily distracted and soon we're disconnected from our heart and our soul and our truest desires—and we don't even know it.

With all the busyness and noise, we simply adjusted to it. We got used to it. It feels normal, even desirable. Indeed, we've come to like it.

Cornelius Plantinga, in an article he wrote called "Background Noise," contends that we have come to so love the noise that silence is a threat to us, so we delete it. We overwhelm it with more noise. "People haul their boom boxes to the seashore so they do not have to live in the silence between the rolling of the surf and the crying of the gulls. . . . But noisy souls, like boom boxes, drown out the sounds of the sea. It is only the quiet soul that can receive the words, the tone, and the timber of another person's voice, maybe even the voice of God. . . . And silence is the primary context from which we learn to listen, creating an absorbency of the soul that not only listens. It truly can hear."[47]

Being still feels like a colossal waste of time, like being a slacker. If you're still, even for a short while, you'll fall short of the goals you set for yourself. You'll get passed by unstill people. Left in the dust. You have big, urgent stuff to do, after all.

"Be still, and know that I am God" (Psalm 46:10 NIV). *The Message* translates this same verse as, "Step out of the traffic! Take a long, loving look at me, your High God." I don't know about you, but when I'm caught up in traffic, my tendency is not to step out, but to step it up—to drive faster and get to the front of the line! Humans are the only creatures that speed up when lost.

Psalm 46 was written over three thousand years ago. Practicing stillness is an ancient problem, not a new one. But we are now outfitted for a cacophony of distraction, not silence. We carry a movie theater, library, camera, travel agent, speaking road atlas, currency exchange, Bible, health monitor, bank, TV, calculator, media machine, and communications device in our pocket—all with more power than what originally landed humans on the moon. It enables us to always be connected, tuned in, turned on, to perpetually stream un-stillness and never experience quiet—if we allow it.

Practicing stillness is an ancient problem, not a new one.

The average American checks their cell phone eighty times a day, and 70 percent of people say they sleep with their phone within reach. Many people sleep *on* their phone to monitor their sleep, and then they wonder why they don't sleep well. Crazy!

A friend once posited to me (John) that "technology is the new idolatry" after observing a person walk up to communion in his parish while covertly working his smartphone. There is even a description of the reverent posture before this god: "Doing the Blackberry [now iPhone] prayer." Here's the problem. Our souls don't do life at the speed of a smartphone.

C. S. Lewis wrote: "The real problem of the Christian life comes where people do not usually look for it. It comes the very moment you wake up each morning. All your wishes and hopes for the day rush at you like wild animals. The first job each morning consists simply in shoving them all back; in listening to that other voice, taking that other point of view, letting the other larger, stronger, quieter life come flowing in. And so on, all day. Standing back from all your natural fussings and fretting; coming in and out of the wind."[48]

In order to do that—to *really* listen—requires you to be quiet. Just as the prophet Elijah learned on Mount Horeb, the voice wasn't in the wind, or the earthquake, or the fire, but in the gentle and quiet whisper—a "still small voice" (1 Kings 19:12 NKJV). To hear His voice, we must be *still*. And listen.

Don't make this more complicated than it is, however. Don't spiritualize it or make it a have-to religious ritual either. Here are some *simple practices* to help you turn down the volume:

- Turn off the radio in your car and invite God into the silent space.
- When you're soaking in the shower, don't sing (you're not that good). Become mindful in the silence of His presence.
- Do as we occasionally do at big sporting events and take a minute of silence and remember . . .
- When you first wake up, spend the first several minutes quietly practicing gratitude for whatever immediately comes to mind before you set one foot on the floor.
- Take breaks from your technology. Enjoy a tech-free day. Turn off all notifications. (You can do this!)
- Occasionally take a break from words. Spend a few minutes, or an hour, or a day in silence. (An extrovert's worst nightmare!) Notice how uncomfortable that makes you.
- Go on a silent retreat like what Dave described in Chapter 5.
- Pick a comfortable place and a time every day when you're alert and sit quietly in His presence.

Man plans, and God laughs. But when we listen, God speaks. Are you hearing Him?

Solitude

This may seem even a little more uncomfortable to you than silence. In a world addicted to noise, silence feels like anathema to most people. But maybe you can get on board with occasionally being quiet.

But *solitude* . . . as in being all alone?

Dallas Willard says, "In penal institutions, solitary confinement is used to break the strongest of wills. . . . Today, sustained withdrawal from society *into solitude* seems to indicate weakness, suffering, flight, or failure rather than a great source of strength, joy, and effectiveness."[49]

When Jesus was led by the Spirit into the wilderness to be tempted by the devil, it almost seems designed to put Jesus in the weakest possible position (Luke 4). But in point of fact, after forty days of being with the Father and "eating bread you know not of," He was at His strongest.

As with John the Baptist before Him, Jesus constantly sought solitude, not as a place of depletion but as a place of strengthening and strength. (For example, see Matthew 14:13, 23; Mark 1:35; 6:31–32; 9:2; 14:32; Luke 5:15–16; 6:12–13; 9:18; 11:1; 22:39.)

Solitude and Loneliness

In the midst of the coronavirus epidemic, we have rediscovered how relational we really are. "Sheltering at home" and practicing "social distancing" felt acceptable for thirty days, but as it dragged on and on, we became anxious to be back with the people we love. Even people we don't love. Just people. Somebody. Anybody! Social distancing feeds loneliness.

Dick and Ruth Foth state, "Theologian Paul Tillich said, 'Language . . . has created the word *loneliness* to express the *pain* of being alone. And it has created the word *solitude* to express the *glory* of being alone.' One is toxic, while the other is life-giving."[50]

We are dependent on relationship. God created us for relationship, but Jesus modeled regularly withdrawing to solitary places to pray. Why? In solitude, we purposefully withdraw from interaction with other human beings, denying ourselves companionship and all that comes from our conscious interaction with others. While the thought of that can be distressing for some, solitude actually frees us.

> *As with John the Baptist before Him, Jesus constantly sought solitude, not as a place of depletion but as a place of strengthening and strength.*

This above all explains its primacy and priority among all the spiritual practices, and perhaps why Jesus did it so often.

Dallas Willard says, "The normal course of day-to-day human interactions locks us into patterns of feeling, thought, and action that are geared to a world set against God. . . . In solitude we find psychic distance, the perspective from which we can see, in the light of eternity, the created things that trap, worry, and oppress us."[51]

Timothy Keller adds, "Archbishop William Temple once said, 'Your religion is what you do with your solitude.' In other words, the true god of your heart is what your thoughts effortlessly go to when there is nothing else demanding your attention."[52] I'm imagining

Jesus' thoughts effortlessly turned to His Father in times of stillness and solitude.

Both silence and solitude are dependent on trust. Do we trust God to be with us when we are alone? Do we trust Him to speak for us and to us when we are silent?

One word of caution here: Being alone is great for intimacy with God, but it can be destructive for nearly everything else. We'll dig into this in the next chapter. Almost every leader Dave and I have seen fail in one way or another had one characteristic in common: isolation. Like strengths overexpressed, this practice overdone can easily become a weakness, or worse, a tragic derailer.

Don't overthink this rhythm either. Here are some *simple practices* for being alone with God:

- Take a break midday to go for a quiet walk alone.
- View time even in the midst of rush hour traffic or a crush of people on the subway as a time of solitude. You don't always have to be solitary to enjoy solitude.
- Wake up a bit earlier in the morning before the rest of your family and quietly start your day.
- Find a place—the library, a coffee shop, chapel, a room in your house—where you regularly go and sit alone, listen, and write.
- Dig in the dirt of your fear. What are you afraid of? Then go on a solo retreat with God!

Sabbath

The Lord has spoken, "If you . . . call the Sabbath a delight . . . then you shall take delight in the LORD, and I will make you ride upon the heights of the world" (Isaiah 58:13–14 ESV).

We described Sabbath at some length in Chapter 5, but want to include it in the context of "Learning to Breathe Deeply" as a healthy (God-commanded) spiritual rhythm.

For many years, I (John) had a parochial understanding of Sabbath. I thought it was merely a day off from work when stores were closed. Much like the Pharisees in Scripture, my understanding was hampered by a religious, rules-following perspective. It was a day, if followed at all, that was characterized by a list of not-to-dos. It was the least enjoyable day of the week.

But the God who made Sabbath is not a cranky schoolmaster, always forbidding, coercing obedience, watching sniveling subjects slink about in cowardly compliance. The Creator of Sabbath is saying, "Let Me make it easier for you." If you work all week and forget to rest, you will become bitter and hard and lose precious

> *Forgetting Sabbath is like forgetting to unwrap the most beautiful gift under the tree. God says, "Please don't."*

nourishment for joy. You will work too hard and forget your more tender mercies, forget those you love, forget your children, and your natural wonder. Forgetting Sabbath is like forgetting to unwrap the most beautiful gift under the tree. God says, "Please don't."

Instead, remember! Remember that everything you have received is a blessing. Remember to delight in your life, in the fruits of your labor. Remember to stop and offer thanks for the wonder of it all. Remember to rest and play, to bless and make love, to eat with those you love, and to take comfort, easy and long, in this gift of sacred rest. Remember the Sabbath day to keep it holy—to consider it a sacred space.

A Day of Delight

Former Senator Joe Lieberman describes Sabbath this way: "For me, Sabbath observance is a gift because it is one of the deepest, purest, pleasures of my life. It is a day of peace, rest, and sensual pleasure. When I say the Sabbath is sensual, I mean . . . it engages the senses—sight, sound, taste, smell, and touch—with beautiful settings, soaring melodies, wonderful food and wine, and lots of love."[53]

According to Wayne Muller, who interviewed several Sabbath practitioners, "One of the more popular Sabbath activities is making love. Indeed, the Talmud tractate on marriage states that the righteous couple should make love every Friday night [to begin Sabbath]. One practitioner told me that it is traditional in some sects to make love four times during the Sabbath. Hearing this, I respectfully inquired as to whether he and his wife did, in fact, faithfully keep this particular precept. 'No, we make love only once. But,' he added with a twinkle, 'we hold a deep intention for the other three.'"[54]

None of that sounds like not-to-dos! Indeed, Sabbath is to be a day of delight.

Rest for the Soul

A true Sabbath, says Marjorie Thompson in her book *Soul Feast*, is not just for rest and renewal of the body but for the soul. It's not just time off from work, it is time expanded out with God. In the Jewish tradition, Sabbath was rooted in the creation story in Genesis. And the creation story describes "day" as beginning at sundown. Genesis 1:5 says there was evening and there was morning, the first day. Then there was evening and there was morning, the second day.

Imagine starting your day with the evening meal, then going to bed. So the first third of your day is spent sleeping—trusting that God is at work while you sleep. Then when you rise, you begin again to participate with God in what He's *already* doing. This obviously speaks to a very different rhythm, because most of us have developed what Thompson calls "a secular rhythm of life in direct contrast to the ancient sacred pattern . . . sacred rhythm of life."[55]

Thompson says to look at it like this:

- Secular Rhythm—begins with work and moves to rest (or to vacation).
- Sacred Rhythm—begins with rest (the evening meal and Sabbath) and moves to work (or to vocation).
- Secular Rhythm—begins its cycle in a mode that is driven by production and achievement, moving typically to exhaustion and collapse, or perhaps to the numbing escapes of mindless entertainment.
- Sacred Rhythm—begins its cycle with an invitation to rest, in the quiet replenishing depths of God's presence, then moves out and gets to work. But the work is a grateful and energized response to God.

Think about that. We often work ourselves to breathless exhaustion, then rest. We work crazy hours in a week, then binge sleep, thinking we can play catch up on the weekend. Five or six days of four hours of sleep followed by a ten-hour exhausted coma. It just doesn't work that way. Binging anything is unhealthy, whether it's eating, drinking, working, sleeping, even Netflix.

What if we viewed Sabbath as rest at the beginning rather than the end of the week? The healthy rhythm is to rest to work, not the other way around. But this is not easy, as it runs counter to our culture. Stores aren't even closed on holidays anymore, let alone on Sunday. Chick-fil-A is an anomaly. Life and work have become a 24/7/365 race to the exhausted finish.

We've bought into this frenetic pace hook, line, and sinker. When our boys were young athletes, one family in our community attempted to begin a movement to restrict sports practices on Sunday mornings and Wednesday nights, so families could observe faith rituals or at least have structured family time. They were immediately ostracized. Most families with budding young athletes viewed this as an ideal opportunity to leapfrog their kids on the way to getting Division I scholarships and eventual professional athletic stardom.

The healthy rhythm is to rest to work, not the other way around.

Sabbath is a specific practice, but also a larger metaphor for taking a deep breath. Wayne Muller states, "Sabbath time is time off the wheel, time when we take our hand from the plow and let God and the earth care for things, while we drink, if only for a few moments, from the fountain of rest and delight."[56]

Here are some *simple ways* to start a Sabbath Rhythm:

- Decide to try one Sabbath—don't change your whole life yet. Check your calendar and pick a day that works for you and your family. It doesn't have to be on Sabbath day.
- What to exclude—what activities related to work, buying and selling, and worry will you refuse to engage in so this day is truly a day of rest, worship, and delight?

- What to include—what activities bring you delight, and how will you incorporate them in your day? Think of things that rest and replenish your body, spirit, and soul.
- Practical things—don't plan too precisely, make it too structured, or pack it too full of activity.

Prayer

Eugene Peterson observed, "Faced with the prospect of conversation with a holy God who speaks worlds into being, it is not surprising that we have trouble. We feel awkward and out of place: 'I'm not good enough for this. I'll wait until I clean up my act and prove that I am a decent person.' Untutored, we tend to think that prayer is what good people do when they are doing their best."[57]

Indeed, Richard Foster suggests that the greatest obstacle to prayer among us modern high achievers is that we have to have everything "just right" in order to pray. That is, before we can really pray, our lives need some fine-tuning, or we need to know more about prayer, and even how to pray. What we really need to understand is that the heart of God aches over our distance, and He longs for our presence.

"For too long," Foster says, "we have been in a far country: a country of noise and hurry and crowds, a country of climb and push and shove, a country of frustration and fear and intimidation. . . . And He is inviting you—and me—to come home, to come home to where we belong, to come home to that for which we were created. His arms are stretched out wide to receive us.

"We do not need to be shy. He invites us into the living room of His heart . . . into the kitchen of His friendship . . . into the dining room of His strength . . . into the study of His wisdom . . . into the workshop of His creativity . . . into the bedroom of His rest, where we can be vulnerable and free. It is also the place of deepest intimacy where we know and are known to the fullest."[58]

The disciples of Jesus had come to see this very thing in the conversations that He had with His Father. So when they made that simple request, "Lord, teach us to pray," they weren't looking for a recipe or a ritual (Luke 11:1). They were looking for a way to be with God—a way to be *at home* with God—the way Jesus had learned to be at home with Him in prayer.

> They were looking for a way to be with God—a way to be at home with God—the way Jesus had learned to be at home with Him in prayer.

To be at *home* with God in prayer. Think about that! When you feel at home, what do you feel? What emotions get stirred? What words come to mind? Can you feel things in your body? Are you anxious or relaxed? Are you guarded or at ease? Are you free to be yourself and share the things you feel, or do you know you'd be in trouble if you ever told the truth? Do you wear your false-self mask that makes others all so proud, or do you take that off at home? Do you walk around naked, or are you fully clothed? (Actually, that was a test to see if you're still reading.)

I (Dave) have a good friend who shared that she had found some of her prayer journals from many years' past and was surprised by how formal they were. She said it was as though she was writing to try and impress God with her poetry and prose. She thought that anyone who read them would certainly be impressed with how "godly" she was. Then she laughed and said that they wouldn't be impressed anymore. "Now," she says, "I just pour out my heart and tell God the truth, and I swear like a sailor—and I've never felt as at home with God as I do right now."

Jesus and the Inner Room

Intimacy with the Father is what the disciples had seen when Jesus prayed, and that's what they wanted—to learn how to be at home with God in prayer. But He didn't fill the air with words or make long speeches when He prayed. Rather, He says, "Don't do any of that. That's what the hypocrites do, who love standing in the synagogues and on street corners when they pray in order to be seen. But you, when you pray, go into your inner room and close the door. And your Father who sees you in that secret place will meet you there—in your inner room" (Matthew 6:5–6).

That does not mean a room inside a house, though some see it that way. The inner room is that space inside you where God by His Holy Spirit dwells. The ancients considered it the inner chambers of the human heart, while others likened it to the innermost chamber of the temple, called "the Holy of Holies," where the presence of God by His Spirit was believed to reside.

The apostle Paul connected all the dots by saying, in effect, "It's not the temple, it's you. You are the temple of the Holy Spirit. You are the dwelling place of God" (1 Corinthians 6:19). He calls it "the mystery which has been hidden from the past ages and generations, but now has been manifested . . . this mystery among the Gentiles, which is Christ in you" (Colossians 1:26–27 NASB). Alive in you! At the center of you!

That place inside you, at the very center of you, where Christ by His Holy Spirit resides in you—that is your inner room. So when you pray, go to your inner room and close the door. And your Father who sees you in that secret place will meet you there.

Gasping for Breath

Finding the Inner Room

But here's the problem, and it's a universal one—most of us don't have easy access to that interior place. Consumed as we are with the hustle and bustle and the deafening noise of the "outer court," we get stuck there. When we do, we lose track of and get disconnected from our truest self, our truest heart, and our truest desires. So now we're gasping for breath, trying to recover our breath, and wondering if we'll ever be able to breathe deeply again.

Here are four *simple prayer practices* that will help you access your inner room—that will provide intimacy with your Abba Father:

- Come to God the way you are, not the way you think you ought to be or wish you were. If you're going to learn to be at home with God in prayer, you're going to have to be yourself when you get there. You don't have to be all cleaned up first.
- Come to God intentionally. Consider "fixed hours of prayer" as Jesus and His disciples did. Use a prayer book or journal your prayers. One of the greatest motivations for prayer is answered prayer. Journaling provides a record of prayers offered and prayers answered.
- Come to God ignorantly (not really, but let me explain). A significant part of learning how to be with God in prayer is to acknowledge that we don't know how to pray. In Romans 8:26, Paul says that we need to know, and that we do not know, how to pray as we ought, but the Spirit does, and He is always interceding (praying) for us.
- Come to God simply. Anne Lamott suggests all of her

prayers are variations on HELP, THANKS, and WOW.[59] In a nutshell, this is her overview:

HELP! There's relief in hitting bottom, in admitting you've reached the place of great unknowing.
THANKS! Gratitude brings you peace and joy.
WOW! Let your mind be blown by the simple and the miraculous.
Then exhale a quiet, deep breath at the end of your prayer as your "Amen."

Reverent Wonder

Reverent wonder ushers us into WOW. It greets the day with the spirit of the words of Maya Angelou: "This is a wonderful day. I've never seen *this one* before." It is paying attention to and appreciating what God is up to in and around you. The result is invariably gratitude and awe.

There was a football coach in the Pacific Northwest who would occasionally stop practices on one of the rare sunny days and have the whole team give God a standing ovation for the magnificence of Mount Rainier, the spectacular glaciated peak in whose shadow they played. He called those "Way to go, God!" moments.

Photographer Jim Brandenburg set out on an unprecedented personal assignment in the fall 1996. He determined to take just one photograph every day for the ninety days between the autumnal equinox and winter solstice. There would be no second exposure, no second chance, no photoshop. He said, "I felt I had to break out of the pattern my photography was stuck in, felt compelled to let go of life's clutter and a world lit by computer screens instead of the sun. I wanted to wander the forest again, to see what was over the next rise, to follow animal tracks in the snow as I had done so happily as a boy. Each photograph would be a true original, like a painting—not the best selected from rolls and rolls of similar frames."[60]

The quest rekindled in him a vibrant passion for his work and deep reverence for the extraordinary beauty of nature. The resulting essay, "North Woods Journal," contained the most photographs *National Geographic* ever published in one feature in its entire history. It demonstrates the saying, "Life is not measured by the number of breaths we take, but by the moments that take our breath away."

Isn't it interesting that a step toward learning to breathe deeply and refilling your lungs is to have daily breath-taking moments? The natural world is illuminated with the flame of divinity. Snap one mental (or actual) picture every day of glorious sights, smells, and sounds in nature—large or small.

> *Isn't it interesting that a step toward learning to breathe deeply and refilling your lungs is to have daily breath-taking moments?*

"For since the creation of the world His invisible attributes, His eternal power and divine nature, have been clearly seen, being understood through what has been made" (Romans 1:20 NASB). You can't help but notice rhythms in nature. The whole earth restarts every morning. Day follows night. Spring follows winter. Death follows birth. As Wayne Muller says, "There is a tidal rhythm, a deep, eternal conversation between the land and the great sea. In our bodies, the heart perceptibly rests after each life-giving beat; the lungs rest between the exhale and the inhale."[61]

Don't overcomplicate this. Here are some *simple practices* for noticing God: Step back. Better yet, step outside. Be quiet. Listen. Feel. Breathe it all in. Look around. God is at work all around you every day. We just have to capture one photo a day.

You don't even have to step outside, however, if you're more of an indoor creature. What if outside isn't your best side? Spend a few minutes just marveling at your God-created body. We are designed to follow a certain natural rhythm as well. Waking and sleeping. Looking and blinking. Running and walking. Sitting and standing.

Mark Batterson adds this to the wonder factor: "The cumulative DNA in all the cells in your body is about twice the diameter of the solar system! According to one estimate, there are thirty-seven sextillion chemical reactions happening in the human body at any given time. You are digesting food, regenerating cells, purifying toxins, catalyzing enzymes, producing hormones, and converting stored energy from fat to blood sugar. You inhale 550 liters of pure oxygen via 23,000 breaths every single day."[62]

Take a deep one right now and enjoy it.

Developing a Rule of Life

There are many options for healthy spiritual rhythms. How do you know which ones to practice?

We're calling it a "Rule of Life." While we had times in both our lives where anything with the word *rule* in it would be met with resistance and possibly rejection, what we're talking about here is not a rule at all—more of a rhythm (or rhythms) of life. Like the rhythm of work and rest, or silence and solitude, a rule of life is an intentional way to identify the practices and spiritual rhythms that work best for you. A rule of life is a way of saying this is how

I want to live. This is the space I'm going to make every day, every week, once a month, and once a year in order to stay centered and remember who I am. Not because doing them makes you holier, but in some very practical ways they provide the scaffolding and space you need for the work of God in you to grow.

As we stated previously, these are not primarily things to achieve as they are ways to prepare our hearts to receive the gifts that God has for us.

Marjorie Thompson suggests that when it comes to spiritual growth, we human beings are much like plants in a garden. "Certain kinds of plants need support in order to grow properly. Tomatoes need stakes, and beans must attach themselves to suspended strings. Rambling roses take kindly to garden walls, archways, and trellises. Without support, these plants would collapse in a heap on the ground. . . . When it comes to spiritual growth . . . we need structure and support. Otherwise our spirituality grows only in a confused and disorderly way. The fruit of the Spirit in us gets tangled and is susceptible to corruption, and the beauty of our lives is diminished."[63]

Structure provides the kind of space and air and even freedom we need to grow as we were meant to grow. In the Christian tradition, the name for this kind of structure is called a "Rule of Life."

Not Just Rules to Follow

These aren't just rules that provide structure, they're rhythms or practices. Practices that in the course of a day, a week, a month, or a year re-center and remind us that there is *Another* who lives in us. To be clear, a spiritual practice is a specific activity that we engage in, that opens us up and makes us more aware of the presence and activity of God in our lives.

Here's the critical question: What are the practices that work for you? What are the practices, structures, or rhythms that create the kind of space you need to become present to the Presence? To re-center and remember who you are, and whose you are, and why you are here, and who you truly love?

It may not be nearly as diffi-cult as you've made it in the past. Being a *can't sit still* kind of guy my whole life, I've always struggled with silence and solitude. I saw the value of it, and I wanted to do

What are the practices, structures, or rhythms that create the kind of space you need to become present to the Presence?

it, but I never felt that I was doing it right. One day I was on the StairMaster machine where I worked out, and I was "talking to God" about this thing.

"Lord," I said, "I can't sit still, but I like to run! So this silence and solitude thing just isn't working for me."

As clear as I've ever heard God say anything to me, I "heard" Him say, "Dave, I'll go with you when you run."

And He did! I hear His voice when I run (in silence and soli-tude—no headphones). That was my way!

What if your way to be with God is in a deer stand, or a coffee shop, or on a walk in the woods? What if your way is to be an early morning candlelighter, or a late-night reader and journaler? Or a midday runner?

One last word of advice: Enlist the help and encouragement of others. Finding and engaging a tribe that will breathe with you is where we are going next.

READ—REFLECT—RESPOND

Chapter Six: Learning to Breathe Deeply

THEME: *Living in rhythms of grace*

READ the following Scriptures:

- ☐ Psalm 62:1–2, 5–8 (NRSV)
- ☐ Isaiah 30:15–18 (THE VOICE)
- ☐ Matthew 11:28–30

REFLECT on the following questions:

- ☐ What kind of internal resistance do you feel to the practices we suggested?
- ☐ What practices feel most challenging, even undesirable? Which are attractive to you?
- ☐ Where and how do you *already* experience a sense of God's presence?
- ☐ What messages, images of God, or expectations keep you from being silent with God?
- ☐ What obstacles might you face in implementing a practice such as silence and/or solitude?
- ☐ We live in a very noisy world with a confusion of voices. What are the loudest voices in your life right now?

RESPOND to the following challenge:

Look back at the five spiritual practices we've outlined in this chapter and begin to build your own Rule of Life. Do it your way.

Get Specific:

- ☐ What practice do you need every day? (What is the best time? Place?)
- ☐ What do you need once a week to stay centered? (What is your Sabbath practice?)
- ☐ What do you need once a month? (What might you already be doing? Make it official—it's a practice.)
- ☐ What do you need once or twice a year? (Perhaps going to a retreat center to keep a rhythm.)

Get Real:

- ☐ What practices don't work for you? (There's no guilt or shame in this.)
- ☐ What might be obstacles for you? (Stage of life/kids at home/ busy schedule/technology.)

Get Going:

- ☐ The practices take time to develop. Don't quit too soon. Dallas Willard suggests, for example, that the proper amount of time to practice silence and solitude is at least long enough "to stop twitching"!

Everywhere we go, people breathe in the exquisite fragrance. Because of Christ, we give off a sweet scent rising to God, which is recognized by those on the way to salvation—an aroma redolent with life.

2 Corinthians 2

We have all kinds of relationships, but apart from family, none is more meaningful than a friendship. Friendship, by definition, is unique. It's about investment and vulnerability.

Dick and Ruth Foth

CHAPTER 7

Breathing Together

"Would you be available and willing to coach Dave?" was the request from the head of the elder board.

"I don't know" was my honest answer.

Carol and I had attended Church of the Open Door for a number of years, and we both had been challenged and deeply blessed by Dave's teaching. But I didn't know him other than that guy who waved his arms wildly and spoke crazy fast every Sunday morning. Coaching is first and foremost a trust thing based on chemistry, so I agreed to meet him for a cup of coffee with no strings attached, just to see if either of us felt there was a connection.

Within ten minutes, I knew I didn't want to coach Dave.

I wanted to be his friend.

I didn't ever want to sit in church on a Sunday and think, *You know, I should talk to Dave about that. When he says this, it sounds like that.* Or, *It probably would've been better if he hadn't used that example.* Or, *Now I see why they felt this dude could use coaching!*

But it wasn't just that I didn't want to be conflicted when I went to church. It was that there was an immediate bond I felt with Dave—sort of a "brothers from a different mother" thing. I appreciated his weird humor, immediate honesty, transparency, and obvious deep and real faith. We shared some similar life experiences. The conversation was unforced. Honest. Real. Life-giving. There was a desire to continue the dialogue after we'd talked. It was the beginning of what has become a wonderfully rich friendship.

This is what breathing together looks and feels like. My experience is that this is rare. You can't manufacture this sort of friendship. It just happens. But it is not coincidental.

A "coincidence" is how God remains anonymous.

C. S. Lewis described these "coincidental" meetings that turn into beautiful friendship in his book *The Four Loves*: "But for a Christian, there are, strictly speaking, no chances. A secret Master of Ceremonies has been at work. Christ, who said to the disciples, 'Ye have not chosen me, but I have chosen you,' can truly say to every group of Christian friends, 'You have not chosen one another, but I have chosen you for one another.' The friendship is not a reward for our discrimination and good taste in finding one another out. It is the instrument by which God reveals to each other the beauties of all the others."[64]

The key is to *notice* these "coincidental" meetings when they present themselves, and then accept them as the gifts they are.

In their beautiful little book, *Known: Finding Deep Friendships in a Shallow World*, Dick and Ruth Foth state, "We have all kinds of relationships, but apart from family, none is more meaningful than a friendship. Friendship, by definition, is unique. It's about investment and vulnerability."[65]

My friendship with Dave resulted years later in this book.

Biodynamic Vineyards

Allow us to attempt to be science geeks for just a minute or two.

Biodynamic winemaking is a whole ecological system based on the premise that a vineyard is one living organism. Everything interacts together—fields, forests, plants, animals, bugs, soils, compost, and even the people who live and work on it. The environmental conditions, especially the soil and climate, create the *terroir*—the unique flavor and aroma of the wine produced.

Diversity is the key. Monocultures are challenging to the plants. Grapevines that are surrounded only by other grapevines become unhealthy and less productive. In other words, in order for a vineyard to be healthiest, it needs to encompass grapes and non-grapes.

My friend Ray, who owned a vineyard in Oregon, explained this method to me. In addition to several varietals of grapes, he planted lavender as an excellent pollinator. The same is true with blackberries, which also served the dual purpose of being an alternative food source for the birds rather than the grapes. Ground cover between rows of grapevines protected the soil from erosion and held in essential moisture. Roses at the end of vine rows acted as the "canaries in the coal mine." Because roses are so sensitive, if he noticed the leaves beginning to drop or the plants looking unhealthy, he knew they were being impacted by disease or bugs that would ultimately attack the grapevines.

Some bugs are healthy for the vines, such as ladybugs and praying mantises, because they eat the bad bugs. Cow dung provided the best microbes and compost the necessary nutrients. Large trees became home to raptors that would hunt the vermin living in the vineyard. Just the right amount of water is critical. The key is to stress the plants to produce the best grapes. Too much stress results in raisins. The system doesn't work optimally if all the elements are not in harmony.

Perhaps Jesus had all of this in mind when a quarter of the parables He told involved agriculture (none included woodworking), and He formed a biodynamic tribe of followers that changed the world forever.

Jesus' Biodynamic Tribe

Elton Trueblood asserts, "There is no person in history who has impacted all of mankind more than Jesus of Nazareth." His revolutionary methodology was to "collect a few very common men and women, inspire them with the sense of His Spirit and vision, and build their lives into an intensive fellowship of affection, worship, and work."[66] Perhaps most shockingly, there was no backup plan. Jesus staked it all on this unlikely, diverse, and unruly gaggle of leaders. There was no Plan B.

If you were in charge of drafting the twelves players with whom you would entrust the task of changing the world forever, would you choose this ragtag bunch of mostly rabbi school rejects?

Simon was a Zealot—a person sworn to violently overthrow Roman rule. We would call him a terrorist today. Matthew was a despised tax collector in the pocket of the Romans—one whom the Zealot would ordinarily be sworn to kill with his concealed knife.

Some scholars suggest that Judas Iscariot may also have been a Zealot, based on his surname, Iscariot, which is believed to be a form of the title *sicarii*, meaning "dagger men." That suggests his betrayal was less about money than a last-ditch attempt to force Jesus to abandon His passivity and step up as a political liberator.

Thomas's spiritual gift appears to have been suspicion.

There were two sets of brothers among the disciples, so plenty of sibling rivalry and snobbish requests for special treatment, such as when the mother of brothers James and John asked Jesus, "Grant that one of these two sons of mine may sit at your right and the other at your left in your kingdom." That didn't sit well with the other disciples. Those same two brothers were dubbed the "sons of thunder," likely because of some anger management issues.

Then there's the fisherman Simon, who became the apostle Peter. Named nearly two hundred times in the New Testament, no other person than Jesus receives this much attention in the Gospels. He was there for all the *big* events: chosen as one of the original twelve disciples by Jesus, the first to declare Jesus as Messiah, the first apostle to enter the empty tomb after Jesus' resurrection, the last follower to whom Jesus spoke directly, and the first to launch the Christian movement on Pentecost with a sermon that electrified 3,000 people, then was soon followed by another sermon that brought in another 5,000 believers.

But Peter is also the patron saint of ADHD. He walks on water, then quickly sinks. He blurts bold affirmations, then pauses to reconsider. He refuses to have his feet washed, then requests full-body immersion. He denies Jesus three times during His trial, then weeps deeply. His spiritual gift was not premeditated action or speech.

In fairness to Peter, he is often misrepresented. Consider that the water-walking account is most often sermonized as a lack of faith. But he was the only follower to get out of the boat, and he *did* walk on the water. The transfiguration is represented as just one more example of Peter's "sock breath." Perhaps his request to throw up three casitas was driven by a deep desire to dwell with Jesus longer. His three-time denial of Jesus was a grave spiritual failure, but he was the only disciple who followed Jesus into the courtyard for His mock trial.

I have to admit that of all the followers of Jesus, I have always been drawn to Peter—unstable, impulsive, outspoken. Great highs followed by great lows. Even fifteen or so years after Pentecost, after experiencing healings, miracles, and thousands of conversions, Peter must be confronted by the apostle Paul when he suddenly withdraws from Gentile believers in the church at Antioch because he is afraid of what the "circumcision party" in Jerusalem will think of him.

I love this grace-filled panoramic view of Peter's life, and the other disciples' lives, because it demonstrates how God uses flawed and inconsistent people (like all of us) to further His purposes in remarkable ways. That's amazing grace!

I love this grace-filled panoramic view of Peter's life, and the other disciples' lives, because it demonstrates how God uses flawed and inconsistent people (like all of us) to further His purposes in remarkable ways. That's amazing grace!

The diversity didn't end with Jesus' twelve closest followers. In a decidedly male-dominated culture, Jesus was regularly in the company of women. He was anointed by a woman. He invited women to be His disciples. His ministry was funded by women. The longest conversation between Jesus and one other person recorded in Scripture is with a Samaritan woman. Women were the first at the cradle, the last witnesses at the cross, and the first witnesses at His resurrection.

The list goes on. Children flocked to Him. Jesus embraced Roman centurions and Samaritans. He fellowshipped with tax collectors and wealthy Pharisees alike. He touched lepers and blind people. Worst of all, He dined with sinners (gasp!).

What Does Your Tribe Look Like?

It's highly unlikely that you worship at a church that looks like Jesus' tribe. It is a regrettable fact that Sunday morning is the most homogenous and segregated hour in America. This is a tragically missed opportunity. When we don't embrace diversity in all its expressions here on earth, we're missing out on God's kingdom!

Jesus' biodiverse tribe gives us a glimpse of the green room of heaven. He gave us a foretaste of this when He made pronouncements such as, "Yes, and I tell you that crooks and whores are going to precede you into God's kingdom. John came to you showing you the right road. You turned up your noses at him, but the crooks and whores believed him. Even when you saw their changed lives, you didn't care enough to change and believe him" (Matthew 21:31–32 MSG). He could say this because standing right behind Him in His tribe were crooks and whores.

According to Dr. Vivek Murthy, the nineteenth Surgeon General of the United States, there are three dimensions of relationship: intimate (wanting a spouse or confidant), relational (seeking close friendships), and collective (desiring a community with common interests). Jesus established friendships with all three groups. Jesus brought together more than a high-performing team, it was a true spiritual community. A deep friendship built out of reciprocal love.

And what was the fruit of this diverse biodynamic tribe? What sort of *terroir* did they create? What aroma did they give off? Paul describes it this way: "Everywhere we go, people breathe in the exquisite fragrance. Because of Christ, we give off a sweet scent rising to God, which is recognized by those on the way of salvation— an aroma redolent with life" (2 Corinthians 2:14–15 MSG).

Nobody on earth is or ever has been as skilled at forming a powerful fellowship as Jesus. But it is vital that you have a tribe that is similar today—a group of people with whom you are breathing together.

A survey published in January 2020 found that 61 percent of Americans feel lonely or socially isolated.[67] There are reports equating the damaging health effects of loneliness to the impact of smoking one pack of cigarettes a day. The stay-at-home restrictions imposed by COVID-19 have surely pushed these numbers significantly higher, with disastrous results in mental health, addictions, domestic violence, and disease beyond the pandemic itself.

Conversely, the Harvard Study of Adult Development, which has been tracking happiness for over eighty years, has found that people who are socially connected to family, friends, and community are happier, healthier, and live longer than people who are less well-connected. The absence of close social connections exceeds the health risks of a poor diet or lack of exercise.

Everything we've written up to this point—God's perfect breath in you, recognizing your bad (false) breath, acknowledging the air that you are breathing, recovering your breath and establishing healthy rhythms in order to breathe deeply—is all for the purpose of ultimately breathing in community and breathing on others. It's not just for you!

How do you go about this? How do you form nutritious relationships and drop toxic ones? Who is your tribe? Why is this vitally important?

Hide-and-Seek

There are two ways to play hide-and-seek. You can play the game with such skill as to never be found. Or you can play like a three-year-old.

When you announce, "Ready or not, here I come," what you're likely to find is the child sitting on the sofa in the next room in plain sight. They delight not in hiding, but in being found.

The healthiest men and women we know are appropriately transparent, inviting other people into their own life. Their pleasure is in being found rather than concealing themselves from God and others.

We've seen many leaders fail to engage others because they lead compartmentalized lives that wall off faith, family, and personal life from their business or ministry persona. They have more than sufficient skill and intellect, but their lack of transparency creates a scarcity of trust. Followers are left to think, *I wonder what or who she/he is really like.*

How do you form nutritious relationships and drop toxic ones? Who is your tribe?

Erwin Rafael McManus observed: "Many of us live our lives making sure we are not seen. We choose the cloak of invisibility. . . . We choose to remain uninvolved, and our love for personal privacy disguises both our indifference and our isolation."[68]

One leader described to me a layer of "permafrost" between the first fifteen floors of their corporate headquarters and the sixteenth floor where all the executives officed. The truth of the organization seldom penetrated the permafrost. It truly can be "lonely at the top," because leadership involves tough decisions. The tougher the decision, the lonelier it gets. Leadership takes a toll. Parenting can too. How do you overcome that isolation?

Born on Third Base

I once had the privilege of working with the chairman of a global company. He was the embodiment of what business researcher Jim Collins describes as a "Level Five Leader"—one who effectively blends extreme personal humility with intense professional will.[69] When he and I co-facilitated executive leadership sessions, he would walk around introducing himself individually to each leader in the room. "Hi, I'm Bob" (as if nobody in the session knew who he was).

When he was in the office, he would walk down the stairs from the executive suite to the employee lunchroom every day, sit with a table of people he hadn't yet met, introduce himself, and then ask, "What are you learning today?" He personified a humble learner, not an arrogant knower. He had just taken up wind surfing in his mid-seventies.

Every time we worked together, I would get a thoughtful, hand-written thank-you note the week after. This man was authentic. These weren't techniques he picked up in a leadership book. This was who he was.

Years later, I watched his son pull up in his chauffeured limo to a similar leadership session, walk in with his handler, and sit down in the back. His arrival intentionally caused a stir. He was scheduled to address the group at 10:00 a.m. When the woman, who was just finishing her presentation, ran over by two minutes to 10:02, he asked loudly enough for every person in the room to hear, "Does *she* know *I'm* here?" As if anybody in the session had missed his arrival.

How had that apple fallen so far from the tree? One reason was entitlement. The son was born on third base, believing he had hit a triple. But the primary reason was that the son was an arrogant knower. He sought only his own counsel. He didn't ask questions because he mistakenly believed he already possessed all the answers. He suffered from the "smartest person in the room" syndrome.

The father, on the other hand, had a small personal board of directors. He called them his "scouts." It was these wise advisors who had helped him choose how and when to lead this iconic company into China and also to hold close to a 75 percent market share in their industry. His scouts kept him honest, informed, humble, and curious.

Therein lies a key attribute of leaders whom we've seen succeed, the absence of which is almost always a contributor to failure—community. Isolation is deadly. It leads to self-deception and bad decisions.

Life Board

We both believe a personal sounding board, or a life board, is a vital practice for every person—leader, parent, pastor, grandparent, or spouse. A life board is a strong support team. They are your own small group of trusted people who offer support, counsel, and wisdom. Life board members hold your feet to the fire of the commitments you make to yourself and others.

Your life board can include your spouse, partner, family members, colleagues, mentors, advisors, spiritual guides, and wise elders. The only thing they all have in common is you. The core work of your life board is to engage, challenge, and inspire you. They provide you with feedback and resources to make wise choices. Along with Scripture and prayer, they are a key resource in discerning between God's desire for you and what may be your own impulse.

They empower you to drop the façade of a life lived in complete order and daily calm and begin to share the truth—the good, the bad, and the ugly truth—about your work, relationships, faith, and family. When things are going well, they don't immediately think you're arrogant (although you may be). When your life is totally in shambles, they don't immediately prescribe therapy (although sometimes that's exactly what is needed).

They empower you to drop the façade of a life lived in complete order and daily calm and begin to share the truth—the good, the bad, and the ugly truth—about your work, relationships, faith, and family.

I (John) have had a life board for over twenty years. During that time, work has been lost, my health has fluctuated, relationships have stumbled, and my faith has vacillated—in other words, normal life has happened! In every circumstance, there has been more than one board member who has had the necessary wisdom for that exact reality. Because of that, I've been able to gain new perspective when I lacked it on my own. Without that, I would certainly have been lost and out of breath.

All of this may sound quaint in an age of Twitter, Facebook, Instagram, TikTok, and IM'ing. The more high tech we become, the more high touch we long for with God and with the vital people in our life.

Eulogy-Worthy Friends

Breaking out of isolation and breathing on others requires more than engaging a life board, however. We must form some truly deep, eulogy-worthy friendships.

I have given one eulogy for a friend so far in my life. I'd like to think that's evidence of not having many old friends who have died yet. Or maybe it's because I've been guilty of what Erwin McManus described as "the cloak of invisibility"—keeping people at arm's length out of indifference, arrogance, or isolation. I hope not.

The friend for whom I had the profound privilege of being one of two eulogists was a former pro football player named Keith Fahnhorst. The first several rows in the parish that day were filled with retired professional and college athletes. It was heady stuff to look out at an assembled congregation and friends that included all-pros and celebrities.

But the real thrill was to be able to easily and accurately describe Keith's life, faith, and relationship with his wife and daughters. His fears and his joys. His successes and failures. Why? Because we had talked honestly and in depth about all those things at many lunches and breakfasts over sixteen years. We had breathed together for a long time.

My goal is to become a eulogy-worthy friend to other people—to know them so well and for so long that I would be invited to give a genuine, honest, and loving account of their life at their funeral. And to know each other intimately and hold each other accountable to lives that would be worth a great eulogy.

I used to believe that some relationships give while others take energy. The reality is that *all* relationships take energy. Eulogy-worthy friendships take a significant investment of time and energy. The ROI (return on investment) is exponential, however, because of the joy received and wisdom given. This is reciprocal. All great friendships are.

Deep Friendship

Dick and Ruth Foth outline four keys to deep relationships in their book *Known*[70]:

Story: We don't just tell stories, we are a story. Eulogy-worthy friends know each other's stories in depth.

Affirmation: The more I know your story, the more I love you. Eulogy-worthy friends assume positive intent in each other's actions and words. That affirmation has a lifelong shelf life.

Covenant: Eulogy-worthy friends have each other's back. Always. They are in it for the long haul, through thick and thin.

Dreams: Eulogy-worthy friends "trust big and dream long." They mutually encourage each other to pursue their big dreams.

Jesus gives us a new definition of deep friendship in His teaching during the last evening together with His closest followers before His death:

> "My command is this: Love each other as I have loved you. Greater love has no one than this: to lay down one's life for one's friends. You are my friends if you do what I command. I no longer call you servants, because a servant does not know his master's business. Instead, I have called you friends, for everything that I learned from my Father I have made known to you" (John 15:12–15 NIV).

The disciples weren't just friends because they liked one another. It's clear that sometimes they didn't. They were friends because they now had a stake in the Master's business.

So is Jesus calling us to the highest standard of dying in order to be a real friend? That is certainly what He did for us, but I don't think that's what He expects in most cases for our earthly friendships. *The Message* translates "lay down your life" as "put your life on the line." Sometimes, this is a physical risk. Most times, the risk is emotional. To put it out there. Don't withhold. Be transparent. Honest. Be willing to be found rather than to hide.

Who's In? Who's Out?

A word of caution here: The goal isn't to be found by *everyone*. Breathing together is not about building a platform or forming up your posse. It's definitely not about being a person who "pollinates every flower." This is about intimacy, not scale. Even for extroverts, less is more here.

Let's look back to Jesus' example. It's interesting to note who He *didn't* choose for His tribe. John MacArthur notes, "He didn't choose a single rabbi. He didn't choose a scribe. He didn't choose a Pharisee. He didn't choose a Sadducee. Not one of the people He chose came from the religious establishment."[71]

Jesus was not just establishing "a team of rivals" as was described by Doris Kearns Goodwin in her book on Abraham Lincoln.[72] He was intentionally and deliberately choosing to surround Himself with people who would challenge Him, commit to His way as a rabbi (eventually), and walk alongside Him for three years. His tribe was both diverse and intentional.

In the Genesis creation account, these vitally important ten words appear: "It is not good for the man to be alone" (Genesis 2:18 NIV). We are created for human connection, but not for crowds.

So how do you go about determining who's in and who's out of your tribe? Here are a few suggestions:

- We suggested earlier that all relationships take time and energy. But the mark of a nutritious versus a toxic relationship is whether you feel energized and enriched by it. Ask yourself before you are going to be with a person or couple, "Do I mentally or emotionally have to gear up for this or is it effortless and natural? Will I have to carefully watch what I say when I'm with them or can I be honest? Do I feel filled up or depleted after spending time with him/her/them?"

- You are genuinely interested in each other's stories and life. The language of authentic interest is inquiry. Ask yourself, "Are you fully present with each other or do the cell phones come out and time is spent scrolling and texting? Is there a robust back and forth or is the conversation a monologue? Do you crave hearing the next chapter of the other person's story every time you meet?"

- Robust tribes are diverse—a biodynamic culture. They have a healthy creative tension because there are differing points of view and life and work experiences. Ask yourself, "Am I venturing out of my zip code? Are my friendships multicultural, multigenerational, and rich in differing life and faith journeys? Or do I tend to play it safe, stick close to home, and have a resulting echo chamber of opinion, experience, and dialogue?"

- There is "courageous conversation." Our best friends and life board members call us on our BS. They're not afraid that leaning into the truth with love will detonate the relationship. Ask yourself, "Am I honest with this friend/couple or do I tread lightly all the time or withhold because I'm fearful that truthfulness will bring repercussions?"

- A healthy tribe is characterized by reciprocity. Ask yourself, "Is there a give-and-take in this relationship? Am I both giving and receiving support, wisdom, insight, accountability, and love? Or is the talk-listen ratio 90-10 percent?"

- More than anything, a meaningful tribe is distinguished by honesty. Ask yourself, "Are we transparent together? Do we honestly discuss parenting, grandparenting, work, faith, and life? Or is the conversation mostly benign news, weather, and sports sort of jibber-jabber?"

> *Our best friends and life board members call us on our BS. They're not afraid that leaning into the truth with love will detonate the relationship.*

Getting Outside the Camp

In one of the most intimate descriptions in Scripture, Moses, the man tasked with leading the entire people of Israel to freedom, is seen meeting with God in this fashion:

> Now Moses used to take a tent and pitch it outside the camp some distance away, calling it the "tent of meeting." Anyone inquiring of the LORD would go to the tent of meeting outside the camp. And whenever Moses went out to the tent, all the people rose and stood at the entrance to their tents, watching

Moses until he entered the tent. . . . The LORD would speak to Moses face to face, *as one speaks to a friend* (Exodus 33:7–8, 11 NIV).

There's a lot going on here. First, Moses went "outside the camp" to meet with God. He removed himself from his routine and familiar surroundings to spend time face to face in quiet conversation. A vital function of breathing together is to break our routine—to get outside the camp—whether with friends, life board, or spouse. We can easily wear our routine into a rut. A byproduct of "sheltering at home (alone)" during the COVID-19 pandemic has been an atrophying of the soul. We've been forced to encamp too long.

The purpose of breathing together is ultimately to mobilize and be of service to others. To bring a word of love and hope for others from God.

Next, the people whom Moses led waited in their tents in anxious expectation for his return. Their experience was undoubtedly that he had something to say after his face time with God. If we just hurry-scurry through the day, only reading e-mails, viewing Instagram, and only seeking our own counsel, we ultimately have nothing impactful to say and nothing truly meaningful to contribute. We end up as Richard Foster painfully described himself when he was only three months into ministry: "My problem was more than having something to say from Sunday to Sunday. My problem was that what I did say had no power to help people. I had no substance, no depth. The people were starving for a word from God, and I had nothing to give them. Nothing. . . . I was spiritually bankrupt and I knew it."[73]

Therein lies one last and vital point: The purpose of breathing together is ultimately to mobilize and be of service to others. To bring a word of love and hope for others from God. If any of the descriptions of tribe, sounding board, and eulogy-worthy friend-ship sound selfish or narcissistic, either we've written this chapter poorly or you've missed the point! It's not just about you.

If you've gotten to this point in the book, we believe that you have a deep desire to not only *have* full life, but also to be able to *breathe* full life into others. Breathing together gives us the vital res-ervoir of oxygen to then breathe into others blessing and life.

Your *terroir* will be an exquisite fragrance—full of life.

READ—REFLECT—RESPOND

Chapter Seven: Breathing Together

THEME: *You are designed for relationship*

READ the following Scriptures:

- ☐ Luke 5:2–11; 6:12–16
- ☐ John 1:35–51
- ☐ Exodus 33:7–11
- ☐ Ephesians 4:14–16
- ☐ Ecclesiastes 4:9–12

REFLECT on the following questions:

- ☐ In what ways do you intentionally isolate yourself? Can you identify why you do that?
- ☐ Who are the people in your biodynamic tribe?
- ☐ Is your natural tendency to hide or to be found?
- ☐ With whom are you a eulogy-worthy friend? What would you share in your eulogy?

RESPOND to the following challenge:

- ☐ Identify the people you would want on your life board and then form it.

☐ Do an honest assessment on your current tribe using the characteristics outlined in the section "Who's In? Who's Out":

    ☐ Energy
    ☐ Engagement
    ☐ Courage
    ☐ Reciprocity
    ☐ Honesty

*This is My beloved Son, with whom
I am well pleased.*

Matthew 3

*When God could do no better,
He created YOU.*

Monty Sholund

CHAPTER 8

Breathing on Others

The imagery of breath and its connection to the Spirit as the giver of life, from the beginning of the story to the end, is not only clear throughout the Scriptures, it is consistent. Wherever the Spirit shows up, in whatever the metaphoric form (wind, fire, breath, oil, or water), things come miraculously to life.

It began in a garden when He breathed the first breath of life. Then it showed up in a valley of very dry bones. Then it showed up in a city where hope had been lost. And every time it did, every time this wind began to blow, people came to life.

So when Jesus *breathes* on His followers, saying, "Receive the Holy Spirit" (John 20:22 NIV), He's breathing *life* on them, because the Holy Spirit is life—He is the Spirit of *life* (Romans 8:2), and the Spirit always gives *life* (2 Corinthians 3:6).

I (Dave) can't help but wonder what that was like—what those disciples might have heard or seen or felt. Was this a preview of Pentecost? Was this their own personal Pentecost? Were there signs and wonders, and did they all speak in different tongues? We don't know. There's no mention of those things in the text, which doesn't mean they didn't happen.

But some other things did happen that are noteworthy. This was the first post-resurrection appearance of Jesus to His disciples. They were fearful for their lives, hiding behind a firmly locked door when Jesus appeared in their midst and said, "Peace be with you!" (John 20:19). He showed them His hands and His side, and they began to rejoice as the reality of Jesus *alive* began to sink in. Then He said it again, "Peace be with you! As the Father has sent me, I am sending you. And with that He *breathed* on them" (vv. 21–22).

What Jesus breathed on them, I think, was peace, because they were afraid. And what He breathed on them was mission—"as I have been sent, I'm sending you"—because they didn't know what to do or where to go. I think He breathed on them the things that were *in Him*. He breathed on them the Holy Spirit. And in His breathing on them, He was showing them how to breathe on other people, which would be part of their mission. "I'm sending you to go breathe on people. Breathe on them the breath that is in you, the breath of life you received from Me. Go and give that life away for free."

But guess what? As amazing as that scene might seem, we've all met people who do that very thing. They breathe life on people. They are inherently *life-giving*. You can feel it when you are in their presence. You feel safe, and you feel energized. You know they have an excess of life (breath), and maybe some of that life is for you, so you seek them out, as the crowds did with Jesus and as wise men and wise women still do.

What if you could be one of those people?

They're not trying to fix you, or control you, or compete with you in any way, but they may want to "breathe on you," and if they do, you may just feel something come to life.

These are the people, says Richard Rohr, who have allowed life to initiate them.[74] They've gone through the struggle of recovering their own breath, they're aware of their bad breath (their false self/their shadow) and don't pretend they don't have it, and they've reclaimed the wonder of their first breath—not perfect by any means, but they're now capable of helping other people catch their breath.

What if you could be one of those people?

Those Little Words

Bonnie and I got married very young. She was barely twenty, I was twenty-one, and neither of us had a clue. But we didn't know that we didn't have a clue, so as with most young couples just out of the gate, we were *blissfully* clueless. Having children changed all that, not because we weren't thrilled to have them, because we were, but the *blissful* part of our cluelessness disappeared. We were still clueless, but now we knew it. And that was terrifying!

It helped that we had friends who were in the same boat, but their advice was for the most part useless, because they were clueless too. It was the blind leading the blind. So we did what all our friends did. We bought books on parenting, we listened to the experts, we muddled our way through, and everybody lived. But even then, when we were muddling our way through, we instinctively knew that doing it "by the book" was not the key. At the end of the day, the things that were actually *in us*—formed and unformed, healthy and unhealthy— would be the things that our children would catch from us.

If we were full of fear, guess what—that's what they'd catch. And while the books we read on dealing with the terrible twos and how to handle adolescent angst were helpful, if we were full of worry, or anger, or a need to be needed, or a need to look good, or if we were just full of ourselves—that's what they would catch. They'd catch it like a cold, as if we'd been breathing on them, because we were. It really is one of those "whether you like it or not" kind of deals. Whether we like it or not, whether we know it or not, whether we understand it or not, whether we admit it or not, who we actually are inside is what we breathe on people.

So when Jesus breathed on the disciples and said, "Receive the Holy Spirit," it wasn't some magical, mystical thing. He was just breathing on them what was inside Him.

Jesus says that very thing: "The things that fill the heart are what the mouth speaks" (Luke 6:45). It's just another way of saying that what's inside you is what comes out of you, and that's what you breathe on people. What we breathe on them comes to them in the form of the words we say—*what the mouth speaks*. Our words, even the little words we say to and about each other, have more power than we know.

Proverbs 18:21 goes so far as to say that "death and life are in the power of the tongue" (NASB). James, in the epistle that bears his name, spends most of Chapter Three marveling at the *power of the tongue* to set the course of a life, to bless and to curse, to influence and direct, to build or to destroy. It's such a tiny little thing that has such incredible influence, he says about the tongue, like how a bit in a horse's mouth (v. 3) and like the rudder of a ship (v. 4) influence what the horse does and where the ship goes.

"So also the tongue," James says, "is a small part of the body, and yet it boasts of great things. See how great a forest is set aflame by such a small fire!" (v. 5). So marvel at the power of the tongue, the little words that we say and breathe on people, to burn things down—"to set on fire the course of someone's life" (v. 6).

It seems we are living right now in a "scorched earth" sort of time, with shouted words being primarily disrespectful, angry, profane, and caustic. That's all the more reason to speak words that ignite fires of love, respect, reassurance, hope, and wisdom.

Breathing Words That Set Things in Motion

The two analogies that James uses, the bit in the horse's mouth and the rudder of a ship, both speak to something very small that influences something very large. "Look at the ships," he says, "though they are so great and are driven by strong winds, are still directed by a very small rudder wherever the inclination of the pilot desires" (v. 4). This is a fascinating analogy to me, in part because I'm not a sailor. I would have thought, just looking at a seaworthy sailboat, that the biggest influence on its direction would be the wind, but it's not. Indeed, any sailor will tell you that by setting the sail and the rudder a certain way, you can actually make progress *into* the wind.

So also the tongue (or the words we breathe on people), though small, has more influence than difficult circumstances (strong wind) in determining the direction of a life. I would have thought, just looking at a person's life, that the biggest influence on its direction would be circumstances (wind—be it good or bad). Not so, says James. Give me someone with very difficult circumstances (lots of headwind), but whose mind and heart are filled with the truth about life and love, about reality and truth, about who God is and who they are, and then just watch that person make progress in their lives. And do it right *into* the wind!

So marvel with me at the power of breathing on people, words that set in motion the direction of a life. Those words are not to *determine* a life, but to *move it* in a direction, to give it a nudge. Encouraging words, such as "I believe in you," "I care about you," and "I think you've got what it takes," can move you in a positive direction. Discouraging words, such as "you're such a jerk," "get out of here," and "you'll never amount to much," don't determine your destiny, but they can move you in a very negative direction.

Think about it in terms as practical as a career path. Perhaps the career you chose was set in motion by a word that someone breathed on you. They may have said something as simple as "I think you can do it," "you're good at that," or "give it a try," so you did. Or they may have said "you're such a loser," "you'll never make it," or "don't bother trying," so you didn't. You didn't try, you didn't apply, and you didn't move.

So marvel with me at the power of breathing on people, words that set in motion the direction of a life.

Or how about that adventurous spirit that some people have? It might be innate, just this thing you have inside, but sometimes it gets set in motion when someone breathes on you. Maybe it was a parent, or a teacher, a coach, a friend, or a spouse who said, "Yes, you can! I believe in you. Who cares if you fail? Failure shmailure!"

For some of you, that insatiable drive to succeed was set in motion by a word that was breathed on you—but it wasn't a positive word, it was negative. What you are driven by is a fierce determination to silence and prove wrong that word that said, "You'll never amount to anything." You may be incredibly successful, but rarely will you be satisfied or settled.

When I (John) decided to leave teaching after a few years and go into financial services, I called my dad. He listened to my decision and reasoning, then asked, "Why the hell would you want to become an insurance peddler?" I'll never forget that. I decided to go ahead with my decision, probably just to prove him wrong! His words hurt me. They were deeply discouraging and did damage. Forty years later, they still have a sting.

So marvel with us at the power of breathing on people, words that set in motion the course of a life. But now marvel with us at the power of breathing on people, words that tell them who they are.

Breathing Words That Name Us

Over fifty times in the New Testament epistles, the writers refer to the people to whom they are writing as being "the beloved, dearly beloved, my beloved brethren, my beloved children," and sometimes just "beloved."

"Beloved, now we are the children of God," says John (1 John 3:2 NASB).

"To those who are the called, beloved in God the Father," says Jude (Jude 1:1 NASB).

Maybe it's just a generic term the New Testament writers use to address the group with a term of endearment, but I (Dave) think it's more. A *lot* more. I think the writers, with great forethought and intent, were reminding the people about who they are. "You are the *beloved*. That is *who you are*! That is your name. You are BELOVED." When the writers would address them as "beloved," they were literally calling them by name—you are *Beloved*.

When that dawned on me several years ago, I became intensely aware in the context of my preaching that every time I used the word *Beloved* to address the congregation, I was calling them by name. Even if I didn't know their name, that was their name—they were, they are, and *you* are BELOVED.

"This Is My Beloved Son"

It's important for us to understand that none of this was random. This whole *belovedness thing* was set in motion, and then became what it became, through a pivotal experience in the life of Jesus.

Jesus shows up at the Jordan River to be baptized by John. The baptism is an inauguration of sorts, signaling the beginning of His ministry, the acceptance of His call, and His stepping into the fullness of His mission. But the most significant part of this event, and it *is* significant because it is beautifully recorded in all four Gospels, is when the heavens open, the Spirit descends, and the voice of the Father is heard, saying, "This is My beloved Son, with whom I am well pleased" (Matthew 3:17 NASB).

> *This is the blessing of the Father, and it is monumental. Indeed, it is archetypally monumental in that it provides Jesus with what all of us need: the blessing of the Father.*

This is the blessing of the Father, and it is monumental. Indeed, it is archetypally monumental in that it provides Jesus with what all of us need: the blessing of the Father. Because of that blessing, Jesus was ready to be launched into His destiny.

I see it like a movie in my mind, but it's not just the rending of the heavens and the descending of the Spirit like a dove that I envision. It's the Father that I see, and it's His voice that I hear. And what I hear is the Father saying with a very loud voice so that everyone could hear Him, because He's a proud Papa: "Excuse Me, everyone! Can I get your attention for just a moment? I have someone here I want to introduce to you! And you, over there, shut up for a second, because this is My boy! This is My beloved Son! And I want everyone in the world to know that in Him I am well pleased. He's the delight of My life."

Timing Is Everything

Now we need to notice that part of what makes this blessing significant, so archetypical, is the timing. The Father is conferring this upon the Son, Jesus, before His ministry has actually begun. It's before He walks on any water or casts out any demons. He hasn't healed any diseases. He hasn't preached any sermons. He hasn't gathered any crowds. He hasn't fed thousands. He hasn't done anything yet that might warrant an "attaboy."

That means—pause to let this sink in—the affirmation from the Father is coming to Him *for free*! It wasn't because He deserved it (though I'm sure He did, being God and all), and not because He had earned it (even though He gave up His divine privileges and was born as one of us to give us breath). It was simply because of who He was. *This is My beloved Son. It's who He is. He is My Beloved Son!*

And that is true of Him every day—on good days and on bad days, on happy days and on sad days, on running well days and on stumbling days too. On the days He can feel it and on the days He can't. "This is My beloved Son! It's who He is."

So What's the Big Deal?

Let's look at this now from a different angle, because sometimes the significance of something can best be understood by considering its absence. In his book *Sacred Fire*, Ronald Rolheiser observes that "a good number of anthropologists, psychologists, and spiritual writers today suggest that hunger for the father's blessing is one of the deepest hungers in the world, especially among men. Without a blessing from above, and that vitally includes a blessing from our own fathers, we will carry both a deep wound and a deep hunger. There will, in effect, be a constriction around our hearts, a steel band that suffocates in countless ways and helps rob us of both color and delight."[75]

Richard Rohr calls the father wound a nesting place of demons—demons of self-doubt, fear, mistrust, cynicism, and rage. Call it father hunger, call it male deprivation, call it a lack of fathering. It's the same deprivation. When positive masculine energy, an energy that can be trusted and relied upon, is not shared from father to son, it creates a vacuum in the souls of men. And "into that vacuum demons pour."[76]

Years ago, a ministry in Minneapolis would annually host a breakfast on the Saturday before the Super Bowl. Athletes from former Minnesota Vikings teams (yup, the team that *lost* four Super Bowls—we are longsuffering fans here in the frozen tundra) would always be called upon to share stories from having played in the biggest NFL game. One year, perhaps in an attempt to introduce some winning stories into the event, a local Minnesota hero was called upon to speak. Keith Fahnhorst had not only played in two Super Bowls, but his team, the San Francisco 49ers, had won both games. That morning he said something that cut many attendees right to their core. Keith said that our view of our heavenly Father is deeply impacted by our experience with our earthly father (or mother). If our earthly parent was harsh, condescending, mean-spirited, or worse, it's very hard to envision a loving, kind, forgiving, encouraging heavenly Father. He did not say impossible, but very hard.

That being true, it makes the blessing of the Father here, at this critical time in the life and mission of His Son, Jesus, of utmost importance. It provided Him with a rootedness and strength of soul to

Can you imagine what those words meant to Jesus? Can you imagine those words spoken over you?

begin His mission. It was the Father's blessing to leave what had been Jesus' preparation (His journey from childhood to adulthood), and then to faithfully follow the purposes of His calling into the fulfillment of His destiny. It was all because when the heavens opened and the Spirit descended, the Father said, "This is My boy, My beloved Son, and in Him I am well pleased."

Can you imagine what those words meant to Jesus? Can you imagine those words spoken over you?

But it's not just the words. It's who's speaking them. It's the father. It's *God the Father*. While we might be able to imagine God saying those words to His Son, Jesus, it's another story when it comes to us. It's hard for me to imagine God saying those words to us. To me.

So let's dial it down a bit. Forget about God for a moment and simply imagine someone you know—a normal human being. Someone who has what we would call "father energy." But if that's still too big, just think about someone whose opinion you care about. Someone who, for whatever reason, carries weight with you, such as a coach, or a teacher, or a parent, or a really cool friend.

God's Masterpiece

The most significant turning point in my own faith journey (John) began as more of a hostage crisis. I had been invited numerous times by a friend to attend a course taught by a seventy-five-year-old man who took students from cover to cover through the Bible in nine months. The instructor, Monty Sholund, was legendary for how demanding he could be, so I had no real desire to subject myself to such a rigorous undertaking. Additionally, as with many "Sunday going to church to punch the obligatory one-hour clock" sort of Christians, I was biblically illiterate. I'd never really read the Book. I only knew the big Sunday school stories and had a rules-bound sort of faith. As a result, I had a genuine fear that I'd be exposed and embarrassed by Monty's teaching.

Finally, in order to get my friend off my back, I grudgingly agreed to attend the introductory session, thinking I'd be "one and done." At least he'd stop inviting me, and I could get on with my life. Just to make that first evening all the more awkward, I showed up a few minutes late to the class, so I had to sit front and center, right under the penetrating gaze of Mr. Sholund.

About halfway into the evening, Monty began to unpack Ephesians 2:8–10. I had grown up with the first part of the passage— the being "saved by grace, and not of yourselves, so no one can boast" part. My immature faith taught me nothing if not militant modesty! But then Monty pivoted to a beautiful explanation of artistry. His example was Michelangelo's Sistine Chapel ceiling. He described it in such vivid detail that I thought I had been transported to Rome. When Carol and I actually saw the ceiling twenty-three years later, it honestly wasn't as stunning as Monty's verbal narrative!

Until that evening, I'd never *really* heard the second half of the passage. Ephesians 2:10 states, "For we are God's *workmanship*, created in Christ Jesus to do good works, which God prepared in advance for us to do." *Workmanship* is variously translated as "handiwork, creation, and work of art." The Greek word is *poiema*, which means "poem" or "God's poetry." Monty preferred the translation *masterpiece* (NLT). That's the game changer. When an artist can do no better, he or she has created their *masterpiece*.

Monty slowly made his way around the room, addressing each student by name and stating, "So what this *literally* means is that when *God* could do no better, He created *you*, Larry, Sue, David. When *God* could do no better, He created you, *John*! And He created you for a purpose. And that purpose is good!"

> *Words create worlds. They have the power to unleash a whole firestorm of passion, potential, and purpose. They can light you up or simply burn you to a crisp.*

Let that sink in. When *God* could do no better, He created *me*. He created *you*.

I was completely undone. It was as if the heavens had opened and a word had been spoken. And that word gave life. I had done nothing to deserve it or to earn it. All I could do was receive it.

One sentence from that demanding and loving old teacher radically changed the trajectory of my faith journey and, as a result, my life. The Holy Spirit-inspired words that evening breathed life into my dormant soul. That moment on September 13, 1994 (I dated it in my Bible), was the first time I'd not only really *read* but also *written* in my Bible. In a moment I went from rules to relationship. From laissez-faire to deeply in love.

That's what words do. Words create worlds. They have the power to unleash a whole firestorm of passion, potential, and purpose. They can light you up or simply burn you to a crisp.

Gas Stations, Greasy Guys, and Hearing the Voice of the Father

Now imagine being a ten-year-old kid. I (Dave) have the weirdest memory, but I think about this encounter so often that I think it's an important one. I was around ten years old, going with my dad to pick up our car from the gas station. It was back in the days when gas stations weren't convenience stores. My dad had brought the car to the local mechanic to get worked on, and we were going to pick it up.

And we walked. Can you believe that? We walked to the gas station around the corner to pick up our car. Who does that anymore?

There was this thing about the back room in the gas station. The back room was where they worked on the cars. You weren't allowed to go back there, especially if you were a kid. But I was with my dad, and he owned the car. So when he went into the back room, I went with him.

That brought me into the company of men. Really greasy men. Tobacco-chewing men. Spittin'-on-the-floor men. All of them belonged back there. They'd earned their spot as a certified mechanic, as an employee, or as the owner of the car, like my dad. They belonged back there.

But I was a ten-year-old kid. So when the head mechanic looked at me as if to size me up, I had nothing to say. I knew I didn't belong back there. But then my dad did this thing. He put his hands on my shoulders, somehow sensing my discomfort, and with a very loud voice—because that's the only voice he had—he said, "Hey, George, this is my boy."

That's all he said. He didn't even tell George my name. It didn't matter. I belonged to my father, and he just said it out loud. Suddenly it was okay for me to be there. I had a place, but not because I'd earned it. This one came for free because I was my father's son. It's who I was. I knew it.

So what if you *knew*? What if you knew it all the way down to the soles of your feet? What if you knew it so deeply that you didn't even think about it anymore? You just *knew* that you were the beloved of God, in whom He is well pleased. It's just who you are—on good days and on bad days, on happy days and on sad days, on running well days and on struggling days too. *I am the beloved.*

Sheep Breeders, Prophets, and Kings

But what if your story doesn't include the kind of blessing from the Father that Jesus got? What if your father, or someone else, didn't see you, or took no particular delight in you, or never called you his beloved? That would be truly sad. What if you never got the "atta-boy" that you so longed for as a kid? Are you doomed to a life of failure and dysfunction? Are you stuck with what Rohr described as "a vacuum in your soul into which demons have poured"?

John and I see it all the time, and it breaks our hearts. Men and women both, competent and caring, serving and giving, succeeding and achieving, but all that energy and activity is coming from an empty place. They didn't have a person who spoke a word of life into them. They're searching for what they do not have. They're trying to acquire what they cannot earn. They're trying to get what can only be given, and it's never enough.

But are there alternatives? Are there ways to fill that vacuum with another voice—one that might provide what an actual father couldn't or didn't? Perhaps the voice of a teacher or a coach or a pastor? Or a prophet?

A teenage shepherd named David had a father who didn't see him. I'm talking about the eventual King David, the Bible guy who had a father named Jesse (1 Samuel 16). Jesse was a farmer and a sheep breeder in Bethlehem of no particular importance, until one day the prophet Samuel came to him. Samuel said that one of Jesse's eight sons was the next king of Israel. So Jesse called them into the house and lined them up.

All, that is, except for David. It couldn't be David. He was the youngest and least significant of the bunch. He was the runt of the litter, and in Jesse's eyes not kingly material. Indeed, it never occurred to him that David could be the Lord's anointed. He truly didn't see David.

But someone did. It was the prophet Samuel. And while we all might wish that our father "Jesse" could see us, what if someone who actually knows what a king looks like does? Someone like Samuel.

Being a sheep breeder doesn't make Jesse a bad person or a bad father, but a sheep breeder might not be the most qualified to see the qualities that make for a great king. But Samuel saw it. And when he *saw* it, he *said* it. "This kid David is the guy. He's got the goods. I like his heart. I'm choosing him."

Samuel breathed on him!

David didn't get a father who saw him or knew how to bless him, but he got a Samuel who did both. At some point, that has to count. At some point, you may have to accept the fact that you didn't get what you wanted, but you got what you needed. You got a Samuel.

Or if you didn't get a Samuel, maybe you got an Elizabeth. Remember Mary, the mother of Jesus? When she was afraid and confused, she ran straight to Elizabeth. She might have had a mother who cared for her, but she went straight to Elizabeth. And Elizabeth spoke a word of blessing, as in "Blessed are you among women, and blessed is the child you will bear!" (Luke 1:43 NIV). It's hard to beat that word. She was Mary's Samuel.

So who's your Samuel? Who's your Elizabeth? Who's that man or woman, coach or mentor, boss or friend who saw more in you than you could see in yourself? But they didn't just *see* it, they *said* it. And it wasn't just cuddles and bunnies, because they pushed you and expected things of you. Sometimes they even demanded them, because they believed in you.

Who is your Samuel? Your Elizabeth? Do you have one?

Who is your Samuel? Your Elizabeth? Do you have one? If you do, you need to let them know they count. You got what you needed through them. You got the father's blessing!

Can you name them? If you can, tell them. Thank them. They need to know that what they saw in you, what they said to you, and what they called out of you meant more to you than they could know.

You need to tell them, but not just for them. You need to tell them for you, as if you're making it official. They were a difference maker. You heard their voice, and it counted. They breathed on you and something came to life.

Who Are You Breathing On?

What if it's not just about having a Samuel or Elizabeth?

What if it's about *being* Samuel or Elizabeth for someone else?

What if it's about being the kind of parent, spouse, teacher, coach, pastor, boss, or friend who is aware of the power of the words you say to bless or to curse, to call out life or to quench it? And what if you realized that you may not be their Jesse, but you might just be their Samuel or their Elizabeth?

"We have not many fathers," lamented the apostle Paul in 1 Corinthians 4.

But we do have Samuels, I believe. And Elizabethes as well.

Our word to you is this: Do not underestimate the power of a word to set the course of someone's life. Your words have the power to affirm identity, to determine destiny, to call forth life. Do not "aw-shucks" this, as if you're seeing them and delighting in them has no power to name. It does! More than you know.

It's not that hard, not really. All you have to do is breathe on them, and then watch what comes to life in them. Even with your last breath.

READ—REFLECT—RESPOND

Chapter Eight: Breathing on Others

THEME: *Your words have profound power*

READ the following Scriptures:

- ☐ Luke 6:45
- ☐ Ephesians 2:8–10
- ☐ James 3
- ☐ Matthew 3:13–17; Mark 1:9–11; Luke 3:21–22
- ☐ Proverbs 15:7

REFLECT on the following questions:

- ☐ Who are the people who over the years have breathed life into you?
- ☐ Is it possible to breathe life on another person without words?
- ☐ Do you identify more with having had life breathed on you, or death?
- ☐ James said to marvel at the power of the tongue to bless and to curse, to set the course of a life, to build and to destroy. Can you identify words spoken to you that effected the course of your life?
- ☐ Do you remember who spoke them? Why did their words matter so much to you?
- ☐ Are you aware of the power *you* have to bless and to curse? Or do you tend to "aw-shucks" it?

RESPOND to the following challenge:

- [ ] If you have a Samuel and/or an Elizabeth in your life, identify them. Say it out loud. Tell them. Thank them. They may not know the impact they have had on your life. Allow their blessing to count.
- [ ] Consider the possibility that *you* are a Samuel/Elizabeth to someone else. Don't "aw-shucks" it. Don't underestimate the power of your words to set the course of another's life, to speak life, to bless. Look around and consider who they might be. They may be closer than you think.

By faith Jacob, as he was dying, blessed each
of the sons of Joseph.

Hebrews 11

Paul confronted death—examined it, wrestled with it,
accepted it—as a physician and a patient. He wanted
to help people understand death and face their
mortality. Dying in one's fourth decade is
unusual now, but dying is not.

Lucy Kalanithi, *When Breath Becomes Air*

CHAPTER 9

Last Breath

It began in the beginning, with what we called in Chapter One the First Breath—when God by His Spirit breathed the breath of life into the nostrils of the dust that had been formed into man, and he became a living soul. More than the animated tissues of a physical body, he became a living soul. It all began with this breath. It was the breath of God. It was the breath of life. It was the very first breath.

Now we're ending with what we're calling the Last Breath—when the Old Testament patriarch Jacob with his final breath (his dying breath) "blessed each of the sons of Joseph" (Hebrews 11:20). And in blessing them, he breathed *life* into them, and he did it with his last breath.

Ted's Double Life

Ted was a wild man. For a full year, in between banging nails and hanging drywall, he entertained our two teenage sons with tales of his misbegotten youth and misguided early adulthood. We had hired Ted to finish the basement in our house. The good news was that he was an extraordinary carpenter. With an eye for detail and a creative bent that allowed him to work with corners that were seldom square and walls that were never plumb, Ted slowly turned our basement from damp and gloomy unused square footage into a beautiful third level for recreation. The bad news was that the project was eventually months behind schedule. What was bid out for four months took nearly a year to complete. Ted was hopelessly overcommitted.

On the days he did show up and work, Ted always came with a mischievous twinkle in his eye and yet another story to tell. When one of our boys would begin describing the weekend misadventures of a friend, Ted would interrupt with "That's nothing. When I was a kid . . ." and go on to recount some prank or scheme that should have landed him in jail or the morgue. Painting graffiti on the highest water tower and lighting a remodeling customer's $15,000 fur coat on fire with a space heater were all part of a vast portfolio of foolishness that he gladly shared. As a parent of two "creative" teenage boys, I was two parts amused and one part horrified by what this might birth in the already overactive imaginations of our sons.

Ted died suddenly in his early forties. I imagined that only a smattering of remodeling customers and a handful of neighbors and relatives would be at his funeral. It didn't seem that this wild man would attract a large church crowd. Remarkably, the church was standing room only. One person after another told "Ted stories"— the never-dull narrative of a life of adventure, probably equal parts urban myth and truth.

What I recall to this day, however, is the story that unfolded about the present that Ted had given to every child in his church. For years he had used his gift of carpentry to craft faith chests for every infant. These beautiful boxes, unique for every child, held the mementos of each faith journey, from baptism through childhood into adolescence and adulthood. As each young girl or boy matured, significant turning points of faith were placed into the safekeeping of Ted's lovingly crafted chests. It was clear that I had seen only one side of a multi-faced man named Ted. He was much deeper and more faithful than the basement remodeler whom I knew for too short of a time.

His legacy was more about faith chests than foolishness.

Leaving a Legacy

A legacy, by definition, is something that is transmitted by or received from an ancestor or predecessor from the past. But it's more than some "thing" that is transmitted, because legacies have the capacity to "live on" when they continue to have an effect on things in the present.

Sometimes the legacy is financial, as in assets passed from one generation to another, for better or for worse. Other times it's less tangible, though infinitely valuable, a legacy of wisdom and love. In some cases the legacy that lives on is destructive, a legacy of conflict and strife.

Then there is Jacob, who with his dying breath—his last breath—left a blessing. He literally breathed life into each of the sons of Joseph, thus leaving a legacy of blessing and life that would continue to live.

Life and Death in Your Last breath

In 2 Samuel 23, it is written of King David that when he was about to speak his final words, *the Spirit of the Lord was upon him, and so His word was upon his tongue.* It occurs to me that the occasion of one's death, especially if you're a person of David's stature and influence, would be a pretty good time to have the words of God upon your tongue, because the words we say at the point of death (with our last breath) have the potential to *live on* in the hearts of people for a very long time.

Our last breath has the power to become a legacy, for better or for worse.

With his last breath, David could speak life or he could speak death. He could speak a blessing or he could speak a curse. In the face of death, he could understandably be full of anxiety and fear, disappointment, and maybe even bitterness, but the *Spirit of the Lord was upon him.* So David took a deep breath,

Our last breath has the power to become a legacy, for better or for worse.

and he breathed *out* his anxiety and his fear, his disappointment and whatever residue of bitterness that remained. He breathed it all out. And he breathed *in* the Spirit of God, the breath of God, the life of God, and the *Word of God was on his tongue on the occasion of his death*, such that when he died, he spoke words of life with his last breath.

Contrast that with King Saul, the predecessor of David. When the prophet Samuel prayed over him and anointed him to be king, he said, "The Spirit of the Lord [literally, the breath of God] is coming upon you mightily, and you will hear from God and speak for God" (1 Samuel 10:6). Then that frightened young man took a deep breath. And when he did, he breathed *in* the life of God and the confidence of God. He breathed *out* his fear, anxiety, and sense of inferiority, becoming, at least for a while, an extraordinary leader for the people of God.

But then Saul's story took a tragic turn. He forgot how to breathe. And when he did, he became full of himself and full of pride. He began to believe that it was *his* kingdom, and *his* power, and *his* glory. Such that Samuel, who had anointed him, regretted having done so, saying, "When you were little in your own eyes, the Lord anointed you as king over Israel, and He was able to use you, but not anymore" (1 Samuel 15:17).

So when a scrawny shepherd boy named David came along with an anointing of his own, Saul couldn't bless it, enjoy it, or encourage it. Instead, he was threatened by it and tried to destroy it. Full of jealousy and fear, with his last breath Saul breathed bitterness and disappointment. It's no wonder that Samuel was so sad for Saul.

Thinking About My Last Breath

There's a Hindu aphorism that says, "The surprise of surprises is that although everybody who has ever lived in the world has died, for some reason, we think we won't."

I've been thinking a lot about my breathing these days. Partly because of the IPF (idiopathic pulmonary fibrosis) diagnosis that I got last year, but more recently it's because my breathing has become more labored. A recent visit to my pulmonologist along with a new round of tests then revealed that what I'd been feeling could be explained—I'm continuing to lose lung capacity.

It's a bit surreal to be looking at the report as the doctor *matter-of-factly* explains to me what it means. There it is in black-and-white. The numbers don't lie. It's official. He called it a "measurable diminishment of capacity."

There's a little bit of dying in doctor visits like that. Not in the ultimate or immediate sense, but every time a progressive disease such as mine progresses, there's a sense of no return. I'm not getting back what I lost. And while I don't think I've been in denial about this disease, there comes a fresh awareness that this whole thing is real, accompanied by an awareness that I need to let go of something—again.

When I was first diagnosed, my mental approach was to continually push my limits—that's kind of my way—but also to accept them as they make themselves evident. It's been an awkward dance for me, because accepting a limitation of any kind, such as I can't do that workout anymore, sometimes feels like I'm giving up. But continually pushing my limits sometimes feels like I'm trying too hard, and I just need to let it go. But every time I do—*let it go*—there's a little bit of dying.

So I've been thinking a lot about my breathing these days, but I've also begun thinking about my last breath as well. Because Jacob, as he was dying, with his last breath, breathed life.

That is what I want to do too.

All Great Spirituality Is About Letting Go

Richard Rohr states that Meister Eckhart, the thirteenth-century German theologian, "rightly pointed out that spirituality has much more to do with subtraction than it does with addition. . . . Spirituality is not at all about getting, attaining, achieving, performing, or succeeding (all of which pander to the ego)."[77] He says, "All great spirituality teaches about letting go of what you don't need and who you are not. Then, when you can get little enough and naked enough and poor enough, you'll find that the little place where you really are is ironically more than enough and is all that you need. At that place, you will have nothing to prove to anybody and nothing to protect. That place is called freedom."[78]

But every time you let go of something—let's start with something small, like your need to be right, or to look good, or to be in control, or to win—there's a kind of dying involved. You know it's true!

Have you ever repented? Really repented? When you can no longer deny that the direction you've been going, or the attitude you've been holding, is wrong—when you see, to your horror, that the "man behind the curtain" is you frantically trying to manage everyone's impression—there's a kind of dying involved. But in the dying—the letting go—something else comes to life.

Have you ever forgiven someone? Truly released them, said you're sorry and forfeited your right to punish them? Especially when for a very long time you thought you were right, and you fiercely defended your position, but then you were confronted with the reality that you were wrong. There's a kind of dying in that. But in the dying—the letting go—something new comes to life.

It's called "Dying to Live," and people who've learned to do it—to let go of their bitterness, and anger, and blaming, and denying, and need to look good and to control and to win—are the ones who, with their last breath, are able to breathe blessing and life.

Several years ago, in the context of my "hit the wall" season, my wife and I went to counseling. I promise you that every time I saw and could no longer deny my arrogance, selfishness, and anger, there was a kind of dying there. But in the dying—in the letting go—something came to life. Our marriage came to life!

It's called "Dying to Live," and people who've learned to do it—to let go of their bitterness, and anger, and blaming, and denying, and need to look good and to control and to win—are the ones who, with their last breath, are able to breathe blessing and life.

195

It's All Just Practice

I received a call that came out of the blue. We hadn't talked in a while, and he was calling to see how I was doing. He couldn't have known that I had just gotten confirmation that my IPF had progressed—a measurable diminishment of capacity. So we caught up, and I told him what was happening, and as with any good friend, he was supportive.

But Ben was not just a friend. He was also one of the elders who helped me navigate my last year as a pastor at Open Door. As you can imagine, after being in one church for thirty-eight years, the process of letting go and finally leaving can be complicated and at times awkward. Among the things that helped was simply acknowledging together that we had never done this before, so let's give ourselves some space and some grace. But it also helped to keep remembering, which especially applied to me, that our primary job was to *let go.*

Now here we were, almost two years later, talking about losing my breath. I even told Ben about Jacob in Hebrews 11, and how I'd never noticed that "with his last breath, he breathed life," and how I'd never thought of that, but now it's all I think about, because it's what I want to do.

Then I remembered, with a strong sense of gratitude, that the last year at Open Door was sweet. Though there was a kind of dying in all the letting go, some new things had come to life. It was all good. That dawned on me, and when it did, I said, "Ben, that year we spent learning to let go as a board and as a church and as friends was just practice—for this!"

Maybe that's how it works. Maybe the people, such as Jacob, who with their last breath can bless, have been learning to let go—of bitterness, and anger, and the need to be right, and to look good, and to win—for a very long time.

Staying in It for the Long Haul

I hate to admit it, but I'm a church geek. I grew up in church. My dad was the pastor of a church. My kids all grew up in church, and *their* dad (me) was the pastor of the church, so I'm officially a church geek.

But as much as I love the church, I have no illusions or romantic notions about what church life, and particularly what ministry life, can be like. After four-plus decades of pastoral leadership, I'm well acquainted with the unique complexities and demands of ministry life. Often surrounded by people who expect us to be better than we are, or just different than we are, it doesn't take much for us to get dangerously isolated from the things we care about most and from the kind of support we need to stay in it for the long haul.

Which is at least part of why, for years, I've been passionate about what it takes to *stay in it* for the *long haul.*

But here's the deal, as I stated in Chapter Two. When I say *it,* I don't mean the *ministry* (the ultimate goal is not staying in vocational ministry or your job or career). I mean the *faith.*

And by *faith,* I don't mean *orthodoxy* (my concern is not about people becoming heretics by believing the wrong thing). I mean being a person who is *full of faith,* and *hope,* and *confidence in God,* regardless of how successful (or not) their ministry, or job, or career may be.

I've come to believe that's what it means to finish well. It's not necessarily about being at the top of your game with high-fives around, though that would be nice. Regardless of how successful you may or may not have been, if you finish *full of faith* and *hope* and *confidence in God*, you have finished well.

And with your last breath, you may be able to bless—to breathe life into the next.

Finishing Full of Faith and Hope

The apostle Paul provides the quintessential example of what it looks like to finish well when he says, "I have fought the good fight, I have finished the course, I have kept the faith" (2 Timothy 4:7 NASB). The picture usually painted by those whom I've heard preach on this text is that of Paul at the top of his game. His nostrils are flaring, the crowd cheering,

> *Regardless of how successful you may or may not have been, if you finish full of faith and hope and confidence in God, you have finished well.*

with high-fives all around as he crosses the finish line triumphant. He's *finishing well* as a *winner* would finish.

But what those preachers rarely do is to go further in the text, where Paul discloses how difficult it's been. He recounts that in his first defense of the gospel in Rome, no one defended or supported him, "but all deserted me," including Demas. A man named Alexander the coppersmith did Paul "much harm." Other than Luke being with him, Paul says he is entirely alone. Alone.

Adding to that, significant portions of the church, particularly the Judaizers, still refused to accept him as a legitimate apostle. So while we might consider Paul's authority unquestioned, and his words inspired, not everyone who knew him "back in the day" shared that opinion. There were many who went to great lengths to discredit him and destroy the churches he had either started or built up.

Indeed, at the end of his ministry and life, Paul had no trappings of what any of us would call success. No book contract with a publisher. No megachurch to lead. No 401(k) and condo in Florida where he could retire. He was soon to be beheaded, and he knew it was coming.

So Paul wasn't at the top of his game, at least not in a worldly sense. There wasn't a cheering crowd. There were no high-fives all around. He was entirely alone, except for Luke. This was the apostle Paul at the end.

But "I have kept the faith," he says. That doesn't just mean he *defended* the faith (though he did), and it doesn't just mean he kept *believing* the right thing (though he did that too). It means that even in the face of what to some of us might look like failure, he was *full of faith*, and *hope,* and *confidence in God.*

He finished well.

None Have Finished Well

Several years ago while I was attending a Leadership Conference, I'll never forget when the keynote speaker, with a great sense of sadness, made this declaration: "Of all the most gifted men and women I ever worked with in ministry, *none* finished well."

None? Really? None!

He was quick to clarify that it wasn't because of moral failure, though they'd had their share of that, and it's often what we think of when we think of pastors who don't finish well. Rather, it was that the leaders were full of bitterness, cynicism, and anger when they finished. Sometimes it was born of dreams and expectations unfulfilled (what they *believed* God would do and didn't). Sometimes it was a reaction to mistreatment and even betrayal (no longer useful to or in alignment with the *new,* they'd been discarded). The explanations for bitter cynicism were never hard to find and often understandable.

When I heard the speaker make this statement, I felt no judgment toward those men and women, mostly just sadness—for them, and for the church. Having a strong inclination toward cynicism myself (I often wondered if cynicism was my spiritual gift), and at times a sense of bitterness as well (my own hit-the-wall unraveling left me looking for someone to blame), I have a strong sense of sympathy for what they endured, but also regret. I lament that with their last breath, at least in the context of their ministry life, they weren't able to bless or breathe life. It just wasn't in them.

Choosing a Different Way

But it doesn't have to be that way. I know for a fact that it *isn't always* that way. Not everyone goes the cynical and bitter way, though they may have good reason for both. Some people finish well—*full of faith* and *hope* and *confidence in God.* Not cynical or bitter, with their last breath they bless and breathe life, because that's in them.

One person who did was my dad. On the South Side of Chicago, he pastored for forty-four years in two different churches, serving thirty-three years at the second church. Respected as a great Bible teacher who made the Word come alive (he once told me it's a sin

200

to be boring in the pulpit), he was known for his message of grace. They called him "Pastor Bill." To this day, when someone occasionally tells me I remind them of him . . . well, it just doesn't get any better than that.

But near the end of his thirty-three years in the second church, a small group of people whom he considered friends wanted things a different way. Actually, they just wanted things *their* way. And to get what they wanted, they tried to undermine his credibility with gossip and slander and meetings in the parking lot after church where they could whisper lies.

My dad's first approach was to ignore it. "I've got bigger fish to fry." But lies and slander spread like cancer, and when it did, a lot of damage was done. I suppose the good news is that the elders finally saw what was happening, got involved, and the truth was brought to light. But it took a very long time to unravel it all, and it took a terrible toll on my dad.

Watching it from a distance was maddening to me. I wanted my dad to fight harder than he did. I wanted the evil to be exposed and the cancer to be eradicated. I wanted the elders to act as elders and just fix the thing. But mostly I just watched him—from a distance.

It's not that my dad never got angry, because he did. And it's not that he laid down and just let the slander live on unopposed, because he stood his ground and fought it. But he never gave into the bitterness that kept knocking at his door. He just never did.

Three years later, my dad retired. And when he did, here's what I know. He finished well—*full of faith*, and *hope*, and *confidence in God* all the way to the end.

Which is why my dad, as with Jacob when he was dying, with

his last breath, was able to bless and breathe life into everyone around him.

What Kind of Fool Are You?

Ronald Rolheiser, in his book *Sacred Fire*, states, "Richard Rohr . . . defines the task of the last half of life to his concept that the final stage of discipleship invites us to become 'holy old fools.' For Rohr, aging and the diminishments that accompany it will eventually reduce all of us, without exception, to being 'old fools.' That part is nonnegotiable, it will find us all. By the standards of youth, health, sexual attractiveness, status in the culture, and productivity, all of us will eventually find ourselves radically marginalized, 'old fools.' However, where we do have a choice is what kind of 'old fool' we want to be. Here are the options: I can become a 'pathetic old fool,' someone who is futilely trying to cling to my youth; I can become an 'embittered old fool,' someone who while fully aware of my age and diminishments is bitter rather than accepting that; or I can become a 'holy old fool,' someone who accepts age and diminishment without bitterness and without clinging, seeing it as a necessary condition for my next journey."[79]

Whether we like it or not, with age (and certainly with a diagnosis such as IPF) we all become diminished. The mind is not as nimble, the memory not as sharp, and we're no longer able to "leap tall buildings in a single bound." While countless people try to keep age at bay with the latest wonder drug or special diet, maybe a facelift and a tummy tuck, we will eventually all be found. We have no choice in this, we will all become *old fools*.

Refusing to accept the diminishment of age, *pathetic old fools* desperately cling to whatever vestiges remain of their youth, sometimes going to embarrassing lengths to try and prove they still have it. Often becoming a cliché, this is the guy who in his seventies leaves his wife of forty years to marry a child half his age, to prove he's still *got it*. But in truth, it's just pathetic!

Then there's the *bitter old fool*. Unlike their pathetic counterpart, the bitter fool isn't in denial about their diminishment. They see it every day, and they can feel it, but they deeply resent it. They're not swapping out their wife or wearing skinny jeans. But it's not because they've "stilled and quieted their souls" (Psalm 131:2), or that they're comfortable in their own skin. It's simply because they *can't* wear skinny jeans. So they're cynical and bitter, still looking for someone or something to blame. They are the bitter fool.

Rohr adds that there is one other option: the *holy fool*, who's come to accept their diminishment without bitterness or clinging. They've learned to let go and live in the spacious place of acceptance and grace. Comfortable in their own skin, they have nothing to prove, no need to be seen or to be in control. They are the holy old fool who with their last breath is able to bless and to breathe life.

Giving Our Death Away

Near the end of his life, Henri Nouwen focused many of his reflections and writings on the theme of dying, particularly on how our death (our last breath) is meant to be our last and greatest gift to our loved ones. He writes: "There is such a thing as a good death. We ourselves are responsible for the way we die. We have to choose between clinging to life in such a way that death becomes nothing but a failure, or letting go of life in freedom so that we can be given to others as a source of hope."[80] Nouwen suggests that at a certain point of our lives, the real question is no longer: "What can I still do so that my life makes a contribution? Rather, the question becomes: How can I now live so that when I die, my death is an optimal blessing to my family, my friends, the church, and the world?"[81]

What is the final stage of our lives meant to look like? How are we meant to live out our final years so that our death becomes part of our gift to others? Ronald Rohlheiser, again in his book *Sacred Fire*, suggests that the final stage of Christian maturity is to *give our deaths away* as we once *gave our lives away*.[82] Because how we live and how we die leaves behind a spirit—a blessing or a curse—after we are gone. Our caskets will either emit a flow of life-giving and guilt-free-ing energy, or they will suck some of the oxygen from the room and hearts from those who knew us.

> *How are we meant to live out our final years so that our death becomes part of our gift to others?*

At some point in time, it will happen to us all. We will walk into a doctor's office and be given a death sentence. Or death will catch us even more unexpectedly in a heart attack, stroke, or accident. In that moment, metaphorically, we will have been handed our one-way ticket to the greatest of all unknowns. And from this journey there will be no return.

And then, says Rolheiser, we stand before the same choice that Jesus had to make in the Garden of Gethsemane. How am I going to give my death over? In freedom or in clinging? In graciousness or bitterness? In anger or in forgiveness? And that particular spirit that our death leaves behind, our last breath to the ones left behind, will be determined on how and what we choose in our dying.

Which brings us back to Jacob, who as he was dying—with his dying breath—blessed the sons of Joseph. Which means, he breathed life into them, and he did it with his last breath.

But what if your *Last Breath* on earth actually turns out to be your *First Breath*?

> *As it is written, "Things which eye has not seen and ear has not heard, and which have not entered the heart of man, all that God has prepared for those who love Him."*
>
> 1 Corinthians 2:9 NASB

READ—REFLECT—RESPOND

Chapter Nine: Last Breath

Theme: *How do we finish well?*

READ the following Scriptures:

- ☐ Hebrews 11:20
- ☐ 2 Samuel 23:1–2

REFLECT on the following questions:

- ☐ What kind of fool are you? Are you more susceptible to being a bitter or pathetic fool?
- ☐ What does finishing well (dying) look like to you? What would be the markers of a good death?
- ☐ Who do you know that finished well? Was there a lasting effect? Do you still hear their voice?
- ☐ What does the thought that with our *last breath* we can *breathe life* do to you?
- ☐ Richard Rohr says, "All great spirituality is about letting go." In what ways do you find that to be true? In what ways do you find that to be weird?
- ☐ What do you need to let go of?

RESPOND to the following challenge:

- ☐ Talk with some friends about finishing well and what they think it means to do it?
- ☐ Identify the people you know who have finished well and identify what things remained.

*The kingdom of God is like a man who casts
seed upon the soil, and then he goes to bed at night
and falls asleep. When he gets up the next day,
he discovers the seed had sprouted and grown—
but how, he himself does not know.*

Mark 4

Epilogue

So, at the end of the day, at the end of a life, at that last breath—what's left? Has anything remained, did anything grow, did anything matter?

People think about things like that when things end.

When I stepped down after thirty-eight years of ministry at Church of the Open Door, it wasn't the end of all things, but it was certainly the end of *something*. To me, it was something significant. Something that made me think about what people think about when things end.

Specifically, it made me wonder, *At the end of the day, at the end of a life, at the end of a season in life—what's left? Has anything remained, did anything grow, did anything matter?*

This is the great fear of many people. It's not the fear of death itself or even the fear of the dying process. It's the fear of nullification—that their life hasn't mattered. That it has been of little value. That nothing significant remains after they are gone.

Before we conclude this book, we want to breathe life on anyone who is weighed down by this breath-taking fear. We want you to realize that is toxic air you're breathing, and even if you've been breathing it for a very long time, you can recover your breath and breathe deeply and refill your lungs with the pure air from God's Spirit that will dispel that fear.

A Parable of the Kingdom

How shall we picture the kingdom of heaven, or by what parable shall we present it?

Parables, as you may know, were among the most common and effective tools that Jesus used to teach the deep things of God and the realities of His kingdom. It's a fascinating way to teach.

When I was in seminary, supposedly there to learn the deep things of God, it was all about learning systems—systems of theology, Christology, Pneumatology, and Ecclesiology. We studied the "Ologies." It was pretty heady stuff, but the point was always this—to understand it intellectually and to retain the information, at least enough to pass the test.

In stark contrast to that was the teaching of Jesus, who taught the deep things of God, but He used parables to do it. Madeleine L'Engle noted, "Jesus was not a theologian. He was God who told stories."[83] Simple stories that a child could understand, filled with ordinary things and ordinary people, such as the story in Mark 4, about an ordinary man casting seed upon the soil. A more ordinary scene, particularly in the Palestine of Jesus' day, would be hard to imagine.

But as is always the case with a parable, there's a lot more going on than a simple story about an ordinary man sowing seed in the soil. This fact becomes apparent with just a little bit of digging. Let us explain.

Scholars tell us that some thirty years after the resurrection of Jesus and the euphoric experiences of the believers at Pentecost, the Gospel of Mark was written to what had become a struggling Christian community living in the shadow of Rome. Far from the confident hope they felt at Pentecost when three thousand people came to faith in one day, they were now meeting in small house churches scattered throughout Rome, quite discouraged by what appeared to be their ineffectiveness and seeming insignificance. In other words, they had lost their breath and were inhaling a lot of toxic air.

Charles Cousar, Professor of Theology at Columbia Theological Seminary, described them as a struggling Christian community, discouraged about the inauspicious role it had to play in the broader society. "The newspapers in Rome were hardly carrying banner headlines trumpeting the successes of Christianity, its overthrow of slavery, or its winning converts in high places."[84]

They were in fact lower-class immigrants, who because they had no social standing became easy targets for persecution. The Roman Emperor Nero had singled them out as a scapegoat for pretty much everything that went wrong in Rome, including the Great Fire of Rome, which left them not only marginalized as the immigrants they were, but "permission" had been given to vilify them—thus the persecution.[85]

So when Mark tells a story about a man sowing seed, and it is seed that grows in secret where no one can see, it's not a lesson about agriculture. It's actually an urgent message, a breath of fresh air, written under the cover of a parable, to a beleaguered group of people who needed to remember some fundamental realities about the kingdom of God.

They needed to remember, for example, that inconspicuous beginnings in the kingdom of God are often part of the deal. They needed to take a deep breath and breathe out the discouragement and fear, knowing that God often begins a "mighty work" with small and seemingly insignificant things such as a seed, even the size of a mustard seed, that when sown into the field of God's kingdom grows invisibly. Indeed, in the parable, it was while the sower was sleeping that the seed sprouts and grows (v. 27), so it grew while he wasn't looking, and he had no idea. No idea at all . . . until the morning.

When Forgetfulness Is Faith

It's fascinating that almost every time when sleeping is referred to in Scripture, it's seen as a negative thing. "Awake, sleeper, and rise from the dead" (Ephesians 5:14 NASB). "Stay awake at all times," Jesus warns in Mark 13 and Luke 21. To be alert and aware is what we're consistently exhorted to be.

But in the parable that Jesus tells in Mark 4, the sleeping is not a negative thing, but a natural part of life. It speaks to a healthy kind of forgetfulness, that when you've given what God has given you to give—whatever that might be—you go to bed and fall asleep. You breathe easily and just forget about it.

You forget about it because it's not a big deal, at least to you. You just did the thing you always do, and you gave the thing you always give. You loved your family again today, and you went to work again today. You changed some diapers again today, you taught a class again today, then you visited your sick mom again today. It really didn't seem to matter, and it's not that big of a deal, so you go to bed and fall asleep.

But you had no idea the seed was growing!

As it turns out, the kingdom of God is a very fertile field. So much so that sometimes we reap where we didn't even sow (John 4:38). And sometimes we sow and never get to see if anything ever grew. But we just keep on sowing. We just keep giving away for free whatever it is that God has given us to give. Maybe something small, like a seed. Maybe something insignificant, like a "cup of cold water given in Jesus' name."

But here's what John and I know and believe: You have no idea!

Sometimes We Get to See

It's John who gets an email from that kid who drove him crazy when he was a teacher. He was sure he hadn't reached that girl. It felt like one step forward and two steps back every day. But many years later, an email reveals that the kid's life had been changed—and John had no idea!

It's my brother, the football coach, hearing stories from former players who didn't have to come back, but they did, in order to tell him in a variety of ways, "Coach J, it wasn't just the football; it was you." He had no idea!

It's the mom. It's the dad. It's the aunt and the uncle. It's that guy down the block, and it's that lady at church. It's that coach who pushed you hard for all the right reasons. It's the spouse who stuck with you when you were a jerk . . . again. It's the friend who kept calling when no one else would. It's the janitor at Bethel College who knew everybody's name (his name was Keith, and I'll never forget his name). They had no idea!

Like the man in the parable who casts seed upon the soil, they just gave the thing they had to give and then they went to sleep. A healthy kind of forgetfulness is what that sleep really is, and in the morning when they get up, the seed has sprouted and grown. But how, they do not know. Indeed, they had no idea!

Sometimes We Have to Wait

And while sometimes you get to see the fruit, most of the time you don't. At least not yet.

In his book *The Road to Character*, David Brooks observes, "People with character are capable of a long obedience in the same direction, of staying attached to people and causes and callings consistently through thick and thin. . . . They are anchored by permanent attachments to important things. In the realm of intellect, they have a set of permanent convictions about fundamental truths. In the realm of emotion, they are enmeshed in a web of unconditional loves. In the realm of action, they have a permanent commitment to tasks that *cannot be completed in a single lifetime*."[86]

As with that struggling community of believers, living in the shadow of Rome, discouraged by the *inauspicious role they had to play in the larger society*—they couldn't see. Not in their lifetime. But they kept sowing seed, giving the things that God gave them to give, and whatever it was that they couldn't see then, they see now.

We get a glimpse of this reality in Paul's letter to the Philippians, when he shares quite candidly, "Holding fast to the word of life, my deepest hope and prayer is that in the day of Christ [which is the day that I go to Him, or He comes for me—my final day], I may discover that I did not run or toil in vain" (2:16).

Notice first that he didn't mind running or toiling. He didn't mind the work. But he didn't want to do it for nothing. He didn't want it to be in vain. He wanted his effort to matter. But notice also that it's not until the day of Christ that he will know for sure—"my deepest hope and prayer is that in the day of Christ I will discover . . ."

Then in the next verse he shares a perspective that helps us understand what keeps him going, even in the context of not knowing what the fruit of his labor will be. "Even if I am being poured out as a drink offering upon the sacrifice and service of your faith, I rejoice!"

Now, to fully understand what he's saying here, we need to understand that the drink offering was something that was offered by the priest at the end of every sacrifice in the temple. After the animal, or grain, or whatever it was that was sacrificed had been burned up, all that was left were some burning coals. Then, at the conclusion of it all, the priest would take a goblet of wine and pour it out on the burning embers, instantly vaporizing the wine, and creating a sweet-smelling fragrance for just a few moments.

I've experienced this at the funerals of a few of my Catholic friends recently. After the benediction has been spoken, the priest will swing an orb filled with burning incense. It's as if the life just celebrated lingers over the congregation for a few more minutes.

What Paul is saying is this: "While I hope to discover one day that I did not run or toil in vain, even if it was just a drink offering that got poured out and smelled good for just a little while—if it resulted in the sacrifice and service of your coming to faith—I would happily pour it out all over again. I will rejoice."

The Parable Is True

Here's what we know. After a lifetime of giving whatever it was we had to give in ministry and in work, that parable is true. And while we've always *believed* it, we now *know* it to be true because we've *seen* it and we've *heard* it. Certainly not all of it, but enough of it to know that the *kingdom of God is like a man who casts seed upon the soil, and when he goes to bed and falls asleep, he just forgets about it. God is at work in the soil and in the seed and things began to grow.*

But most of the time, we had no idea!

And neither will you!

Just cast the seed that God has given you to give, insignificant though you think it might be, and then just go to bed. Breathe deeply, breathe easily, and forget about it. Then, when you're awakened in the morning, you'll discover that the seed has sprouted and grown. And you had no idea!

So at the end of the day, at the end of a life, at the end of it all—what's left? Has anything remained, did anything grow, did anything matter?

Yes, it did! And yes, it does! It *eternally* does!

Breathe that in deeply, let it fill your lungs, and live in peace.

Therefore, my beloved brethren, be steadfast, immovable, always abounding in the work of the Lord, knowing that your toil is not in vain in the Lord.

1 Corinthians 15:58 NASB

A Prayer for Your Breath

by Lance Wubbels

"What is *your* life?"
    asked James, the brother of Jesus.

"*You are a mist,*" said he,
    "that appears for a little while
    and then vanishes."

The sweet psalmist David couldn't help but wonder,

"O Lord, what is man that You care for him,
    the son of man that You think of him?
Man is like a breath;
    His days are like a *fleeting shadow.*"

"Life is…"
    the Bible says,

    "*but a breath.*"

Lord Jesus,

    If my life is but a *mist,*

I pray that you will use it
to water the earth
and bring blessing to others
who share this brief breath with me.

If my life is a *shadow*, however fleeting,
may others be refreshed
within the shelter of my shade.

If my life is but a *breath*,
I pray it will be life-giving . . .
not depleted on selfish ambition, jealousy, and anger.

I come to You, O God,

as an empty breath,
nothing more, nothing less.

Precious Father,
Holy Spirit,

fill my breath with
the sweet fragrance of your Son,
Jesus Christ.[87]

For additional resources, visit
www.gaspingforbreathbook.com
and
www.thingsthatremain.org

Endnotes

1 Annie Dillard, *The Writing Life* (New York: Harper & Row, 1989), 67–68.

2 Cynthia Bourgeault, *Chanting the Psalms* (Boston: New Seeds Books, 2006), 76.

3 Mark Batterson, *Primal* (Colorado Springs: Multnomah, 2009), 76.

4 Richard J. Foster, *Celebration of Discipline* (New York: HarperCollins, 1998), v.

5 C. S. Lewis, *The Last Battle* (New York: HarperCollins, 1956, 1984), 210–211.

6 Richard Rohr, "All Language Is Metaphor" (11 Jan. 2017), https://cac.org/all-language-is-metaphor-2017-01-11/. Accessed 22 Sept. 2020.

7 Richard Rohr, *Immortal Diamond* (Hoboken, NJ: Jossey-Bass, 2013), 75.

8 Anne Lamott, *Help, Thanks, Wow: The Three Essential Prayers* (New York: Riverhead Books, 2012), 14.

9 Barna Group, *The State of Pastors* (Ventura, CA: Barna Group, 2017), 11.

10 Jim Harter, "Employee Engagement on the Rise in the U.S." (26 Aug. 2018), https://news.gallup.com/poll/241649/employee-engagement-rise.aspx. Accessed 23 Sept. 2020.

11 Brennan Manning, *The Furious Longing of God* (Colorado Springs: David C. Cook, 2009), 77.

12 Philip Yancey, *What's So Amazing about Grace?* (Grand Rapids: Zondervan, 1997), 52.

13 John Busacker, *Dare to Answer: 8 Questions That Awaken Your Faith* (Nashville: Worthy Inspired, 2015).

14 Richard Rohr, *Falling Upward* (Hoboken, NJ: Jossey-Bass, 2011), 128.

15 Belden Lane, *Backpacking with the Saints* (New York: Oxford University Press, 2014), 56.

16 David Brooks, *The Second Mountain* (New York: Random House, 2019), 42.

17 John Eldredge, *Wild at Heart Revised and Updated* (Nashville: Thomas Nelson, 2011), 54.

18 David G. Benner, *The Gift of Being Yourself* (Downers Grove, IL: InterVarsity Press, 2015), 72.

19 Thomas Merton, *New Seeds of Contemplation* (New York: New Directions Paperback, 2007), 34.

20 Benner, op. cit., 74.

21 Merton, op. cit., 35.

22 Judith Hougen, *Transformed into Fire* (Grand Rapids: Kregel Publications, 2002), 58–59.

23 Benner, op. cit., 60.

24 Frederick Buechner, *Secrets in the Dark* (New York: HarperSanFrancisco, 2007), 161.

25 Henri Nouwen, *Abba's Child* (Colorado Springs: NavPress, 2015), 41.

26 Harry Emerson Fosdick, *The Meaning of Service* (New York: Abingdon Press, 1920), 67.

27 David Foster Wallace, "2005 Kenyon Commencement Address" (21 May 2005), https://web.ics.purdue.edu/~drkelly/DFWKenyonAddress2005.pdf. Accessed 9 Sept. 2020.

28 Andy Crouch, "It's Time to Reckon with Celebrity Power" (24 Mar. 2018), https://www.thegospelcoalition.org/article/time-reckon-celebrity-power/. Accessed 25 Sept. 2020.

29 John Ortberg, *Soul Keeping* (Grand Rapids: Zondervan, 2014), 43.

30 Parker Palmer, *A Hidden Wholeness* (San Francisco: Jossey-Bass, 2004), 58–59.

[31] Jim Loehr and Tony Schwartz, *The Power of Full Engagement* (New York: Free Press, 2003), 3.

[32] Jared Sandberg, "Yes, Sell All My Stocks. No, the 3:15 from JFK. And Get Me Mr. Sister" (12 Sept. 2016), https://www.wsj.com/articles/SB115801096324259803. Accessed 26 Sept. 2020.

[33] Gary Haugen, "The Top 100 Quotes from This Year's Global Leadership Summit," https://churchleaders.com/news/380269-the-top-100-quotes-from-global-leadership-summit-2020.html/3. Accessed 26 Sept. 2020.

[34] Richard J. Foster, *Freedom of Simplicity* (New York: Harper One, 2005), 5.

[35] Wayne Muller, *Sabbath: Finding Rest, Renewal, and Delight in Our Busy Lives* (New York: Bantam Books, 1999), 20.

[36] Richard Rohr, "Path of Descent" (18 Oct. 2016), https://cac.org/jesus-invitation-follow-2016-10-18/. Accessed 28 Sept. 2020.

[37] Richard Rohr, *Adam's Return* (New York: Crossroad Publishing Company, 2016), 137.

[38] Richard Rohr, "Gazing upon the Mystery" (21 Oct. 2018), https://cac.org/gazing-upon-the-mystery-2018-10-21/. Accessed 28 Sept. 2020.

[39] To the best of our knowledge, the original source of this quote is Henri Nouwen. For more information on his writings, please visit www.henrinouwen.org.

[40] Brian Zahnd, "Twenty-two Days" (17 Jan. 2018), https://brianzahnd.com/2018/01/twenty-two-days/. Accessed 28 Sept. 2020.

[41] Patrik Edblad, "How to Breathe Properly—A (Surprisingly Important) Complete Guide," https://patrikedblad.com/habits/how-to-breathe/. Accessed 28 Sept. 2020.

[42] Ibid.

[43] Dallas Willard, *Eternal Living* (Downers Grove, IL: InterVarsity Press, 2015), 46.

[44] Excerpts from this book's first chapter.

[45] Dallas Willard, *The Spirit of Disciplines* (New York: HarperSanFrancisco, 1988), 6.

[46] David G. Benner, *Desiring God's Will* (Downers Grove, IL: InterVarsity Press, 2015), 49.

[47] Cornelius Plantinga, "Background Noise," *Christianity Today* (17 July 1995), 42.

[48] C. S. Lewis, *Mere Christianity* (New York: HarperCollins, 1952), 198.

[49] Willard, op. cit., 101.

[50] Dick and Ruth Foth, *Known: Finding Deep Friendship in a Shallow World* (New York: Waterbrook, 2017), 18.

[51] Willard, op. cit., 160–161.

[52] Timothy Keller, *Counterfeit Gods* (New York: Penguin Books, 2016), 168.

[53] Joe Lieberman, *The Gift of Rest: Rediscovering the Beauty of the Sabbath* (New York: Howard Books, 2011), 3.

[54] Muller, op. cit., 31.

[55] Marjorie Thompson, *Soul Feast* (Louisville: Westminster John Knox Press, 2015), 72.

[56] Muller, op. cit., 8.

[57] Eugene Peterson, *The Message* (Colorado Springs: NavPress, 1995), 550.

[58] Richard Foster, *Prayer: Finding the Heart's True Home* (New York: HarperSanFranciso, 1992), 1–2.

[59] Anne Lamott, *Help, Thanks, Wow: The Three Essential Prayers* (New York: Riverhead Books, 2012).